Boats and Bait

Wisdom from the Waves

by

Ken Pippin

ISBN-13: 978-1727397321

D & L Publications

Dedication

This book would not have been possible without the efforts and assistance of two very important people in my life. First and foremost, I want to thank my wife, Susan, for the many days she was willing to allow me to leave early in the morning, heading west out into the Gulf of Mexico, to who knows where. She then waited patiently for my return, knowing I would have a strong fish smell, and clothes that would need a real washing before being used again. Of course, she also learned that I would bring home fresh fish. We recently celebrated fifty years of marriage. Susan has also been the one to encourage me to compile these thoughts, and put them in book form. Thank you, Susan, for your love and patience, and standing by me over these fifty plus years.

I also want to express my thanks to my dad, who is now with the Lord, who spent countless hours with me and my brothers in an old boat, and with fishing gear that would never find itself on most boats today. His life was always a constant example of what a father and husband should be. His love for us, and his love for fishing, was a significant part of my development, and the fact that I committed my life to the Lord at an early age.

I have come to understand that if our lives are to mean anything, we must always recognize and appreciate the significant investment others have made in them. I have been blessed to have family, and many other wonderful people, who were willing to make that kind of investment in my life. The journey is always easier when you have family and friends along to help you smooth out the rough places.

Thanks, Susan, Dad, family and friends!!

Endorsements

"*Boats and Bait* is a devotional that has been years in the making! The moment you begin reading one of Ken's real life illustrations of fishing in the waters off Florida's West coast, you are hooked. Ken has a way of drawing you into one of his fish tales, revealing an area of spiritual need, then leave you with a practical biblical insight to apply to your life. I highly recommend *Boats and Bait* as a man's devotional. Truth is, you don't have to be a man, or even like fishing, for it to reel you in!"

John Hensel
Men's Ministries Director
Peninsular Florida District of the Assemblies of God

"Ken Pippin is a person that connects with people the same way Jesus did...by telling stories and offering truth that satisfies and speaks into their lives. I always love reading Ken's social media posts, and I have shared them often. Now that they are available in a book, I look forward to sharing them with even more people. Outdoor enthusiasts will love getting their hooks into this!"

Jeff Arp
Lead Pastor/Kirksville Assembly of God
Kirksville, Missouri
Men's Ministries Director
Northern Missouri District Council of the Assemblies of God

"The best lessons of life involve the real stories that we all continually experience. Ken Pippin, having spent considerable time on his fishing boat, has woven together some very thought-provoking analogies from a captain's perspective. He has delivered an excellent devotional resource that brings outdoor thinking indoors."

Randy Brock
Associate Pastor, Victory Church
Lakeland, Florida

"It's not hard to tell just how much Ken loves to go out on his boat named "Never on Sunday." I have had the most enjoyable times while out on his boat, and many other opportunities spending time with him on other occasions. I love how he takes his fishing outings, and the many experiences he has had while out on his boat, and ties them into normal everyday life occurrences that we may face or deal with. He takes his stories and utilizes their practical principles to encourage others in their walk of faith with Christ. The stories are not only real, but they will hold your interest and provide an enjoyable read."

Ron Henderson
Lead Pastor/Eagle Lake Assembly of God
Eagle Lake, Florida

"Ken Pippin inspires us with his practical, yet thought-provoking, collection of stories. These true stories show us that God is in the details, and also helps us realize there is a bigger lesson found in life's experiences. Prepare to be challenged, motivated, encouraged, and even laugh, as you turn through the pages of this unique and interesting devotional."

Jamie Jones
Author/*The Left-Handed Warrior*
Lead Pastor/Trinity Church
Deltona, Florida

"It is an honor to introduce to you a wonderful pastor, writer, and friend, Ken Pippin. We met through two common interests...Jesus and fishing. Ken has the unique ability to take from the ordinary circumstances that he experiences in life, and communicate biblical truth that helps connect the reader to Christ. Just as Jesus used parables, Ken's use of illustrations brings focus of the eternal to our awareness, and causes us to think in terms of the reality of the invisible realm of faith. Ken's love for people is genuine, and his concern for their spiritual growth is easily seen through the devotionals that he writes. I heartily recommend this book for those who want to discover God in the normal everyday events of life."

Pastor Larry Kessler has been ordained with the Assemblies of God for 40 years, and has pastored for 32 years, involved in church planting and revitalization. He and his wife, Mary, founded Joshua Unlimited, serving in Russia for over 25 years, preaching, teaching, and planting new churches, alongside the national church, the Union of Evangelistic Churches. They rotate in and out of the country every 90 days; while in the United States, they help resource Ministries in Appalachia, and support Home Missions projects.

"Having the honor of serving under Pastor Ken Pippin's leadership for over 12 years I have realized the depth of his spiritual understanding. He has a great gift for connecting the Word of God with relatable life events. If you are looking for an understandable way to connect the great and deep spiritual truths in God's Word with life-changing application, this book is for you."

Joshua Morales
Lead Pastor/Trinity Church
Tarpon Springs, Florida

"I am privileged to know Pastor Ken Pippin, and the wonderful things he is doing through the 'Finish Strong' ministry of the Peninsular Florida District of the Assemblies of God. Pastor Ken Pippin shows us how to open our eyes to the miraculous in everyday 'fishing' stories. This book is bound to stoke the fire of your faith."

Rev. Bill Hartman
Lead Pastor/Christian Life Assembly of God
Ocala, Florida

"Ken Pippin's stories masterfully connects readers to his love for fishing by reeling you in through experiences, whether it is nearly losing his life at sea or struggling to pull in that fish that would love to be "the one that got away." Ken skillfully connects his real life personal experiences to guide believers in spiritual truths that bring them into a closer knowledge of the Father's heart. Colossians 3:17 says, 'And whatever you do, in word or deed, do everything in the name of the Lord Jesus, giving thanks to God the Father through Him.'"

Jeff Jennings
Lead Pastor/Florida City First Assembly
Florida City, Florida

"I have always been recharged by any kind of fishing, anywhere. I enjoy every part of the process. You prepare your gear, you wait for the perfect moment to set the hook, and then enjoy the process necessary to win the catch. Whether you land your limit, or get skunked, there's always something rewarding along the way. That's what draws me to Ken's stories over and over. He prepares me with a real life fishing or boating scenario I can relate to. He sets the hook we both felt when things went perfectly, or maybe not so perfectly, then, he reels me in with the message that God wants us all to remember. It's a great way to escape on a fishing or boating trip that always ends in us catching something we're fishing for. Whether you like to fish or not, I hope you will allow yourself to escape into Ken's book, and draw closer to our Savior who loves you."

Bruce Gane
EHS Director
Magne Gas Corporation

"Within the pages of this book, Ken Pippin presents some great lessons that are practical to everyday life. Being a Christian isn't always easy, but if you're willing to get your clothes wet and your hands dirty, the bountiful rewards come swimming right in. Pastor Ken walks us through these delicate life experiences, and provides wisdom to learn as much from your failures as you do from your successes. With his guidance, we see how to reach our prize with dignity and integrity."

David Houck
US Missions

“Both boating and fishing are passions in Ken Pippin’s life. Not only is he a great fisherman and experienced navigator on the water, he is an excellent teacher of life. *Boats and Bait* will be welcome reading that will provide helpful insights to make your water experiences much better. Each short story will warm your heart, and add a splash of wisdom to assist you in untangling your life. I’m certain this book will awaken something deep down inside of you. As you thoughtfully reflect on each story, you may sense that it’s the start of something really important in your life.”

Russ DeBord
Lead Pastor/Miami Sunset Chapel Assembly of God

Foreword

Ken Pippin has a unique ability to take his personal experiences, and write about them in a way that captivates you. When I first read one of Ken's fishing stories, I felt like I was on the boat with him. I was caught up in every word, every detail, and every description of what Ken was feeling while on the boat. I did not realize I was reading a devotion. I thought I was reading a fishing story. He then took what was happening on the boat and applied it to our Christian walk. The impact was incredible. The writing was so vivid; it was etched in my mind forever.

As you read each of these personal encounters, you will get so caught up in the story you will forget, as well, that you are reading a devotion. That's when it happens. He totally turns the story into a life-provoking word that has the ability to change how you think about your walk with the Lord.

I saw Ken at a recent minister's meeting, and asked if he had his devotions put together in a book. His answer surprised me when he said no. I challenged him to put these devotions in a collection, and that is exactly what he has done. The stories you are about to read are part of that collection of stories I have read over the years, posted on his Facebook page. Get ready to be challenged, inspired, and learn.

You will never go fishing again without thinking about one of Ken's stories and the life application. You will begin to see the things that happen in your day-to-day life are not just happening by coincidence. They are God-moments. They are moments that have deep spiritual meaning. Enjoy these moments and ponder on them. Like Ken's life stories, they will change your life. I pray that God will open our eyes that we may be able to see Him in our everyday lives.

Imagine what could happen if you would start sharing your stories with others who may not know Jesus. Ken certainly sets the bar high for us, but the point is that people love to hear your life stories.

This is not just another devotional book that you will read for a couple of days, and then put it down. This will be a book that you remember for years to come. I believe it will change how you see your own life stories.

Ken is not just another person who writes devotions. He is a devoted follower of Jesus Christ and a mighty servant of God. As you will see in his writings, his life speaks for itself.

Pastor Terry L. Howell
Lead Pastor
Living Water Fellowship
Kissimmee, FL

Introduction

I've often wondered why it was in the plan of God for Jesus to choose four fishermen to be disciples. He chose Peter, his brother, Andrew, and, also, another brother duo, James and John. Out of twelve disciples, one third were fishermen. No matter how long we speculate on that question, our conclusions will only be just that, speculation. For myself, I like to think that Jesus knew that the Gospel work would closely resemble the occupation of fishing, so much so that Jesus says in Matthew 4:19, "Come, follow me, and I will send you out to fish for people."

In the pages of this book, I have compiled a number of stories about things I have personally experienced in my life, either on a boat, or enjoying my favorite sport of fishing. In each incident, the Holy Spirit has taught me principles that can be easily applied to our relationship with Christ. As you read each story, you may find another principle or two that I may not have seen, or at least did not have room to incorporate at this particular time.

My intent in putting this collection of stories together is to place within your grasp easy to read and understand truths that are not only Biblically based, but can be easily applied to your life. Even if you are not a boater, or fishing enthusiast, I believe you will find, in the pages of this book, humor, wisdom, and solid truth that will challenge you in your relationship with Christ and the world around you.

I trust as you read through this book, either as a daily part of your devotional time, or just to spend some time listening to the Holy Spirit, that your life and relationship with Christ will grow and be challenged. I believe the Holy

Spirit will help you to see yourself in many of these stories, and they will open your heart to a new sensitivity to His voice in your life.

The enemy is constantly seeking to kill, steal, and destroy in our lives and testimonies for Christ. It is only as we learn to apply Biblical truths and principles to our lives that we can mount a defense that will defeat his attacks. To refuse to engage the enemy in an offensive action is to surrender to his deception against you. We have been made more than a conqueror in Christ, but that is not a promise if we fail to utilize the weapons that Christ has entrusted to us. When we arm ourselves with the spiritual weapons of the Holy Spirit, we can defeat the enemy and help guide others into that same kind of victory.

As a pastor for over thirty-two years, and now the Director of Finish Strong Ministries with the Peninsular Florida District Council of the Assemblies of God, I have had the privilege of working in the Kingdom of God. I know from firsthand experience that there is no greater joy than to know that your life is in the perfect will of God.

These are things that happened in my life to teach me a timely spiritual truth. I am sure you also have many stories in your life that have also been used by the Holy Spirit to teach you powerful Biblical principles!

My prayer for you, as you open these pages, is the statement found in 3 John 1:4, "Nothing could make me happier than getting reports that my children continue diligently in the way of Truth!"

God bless you as you read and grow in Christ!

Apply the Belt of Truth

While fishing on Good Friday with our soundman and his eighteen-year-old son, Zack, the drag on my large grouper rod began to signal a fish had hit. I quickly set the hook, and immediately realized the fish had to be well over 100 pounds. I turned to Zack, who was behind me, and asked him if he wanted to come and fight the fish. There was no hesitation, as he stepped up and took the rod. He could not believe how powerful the fish was, and was having a difficult time holding the rod with one hand and trying to turn the reel with the other. I reached for the fighting belt I had in the boat, and placed it around his waist. With something to firmly rest the rod butt in, he now began to gain the upper hand on the huge fish.

We live in a world that has little concern for the truth. Often we face situations that seem to be more than we can deal with, especially when things are being said that do not reflect Biblical truth. Let me encourage you that no matter how much weight the enemy seems to be pushing around, the belt of God's truth will always allow you to gain an upper hand in the contest. We can overcome evil with the good of God's truth.

By the way, we got the eight-foot nurse shark close enough to the boat we could touch it, and it would have easily tipped the scales at better than 150 pounds. Great job, Zack!

Let's always be assured we can wear the belt of God's truth with confidence.

Ephesians 6:14, "Stand firm then, with the belt of truth buckled around your waist."

Attracting the Enemy

We were in Florida City for the weekend to perform a wedding for our former Youth Pastor's daughter. While there, Susan and I were privileged to stay one night in Marathon at a beautiful condo. When we walked out on the dock that was on the Gulf, we noticed several large tarpon swimming under the dock. I wondered why they were so close to the shore and people. The next morning, when I went down early, I noticed one of the fishing guides was throwing dead fish into the water. Suddenly, the tarpon were in a feeding frenzy. Then I knew why they were there; they were expecting to be fed.

That picture brought a thought to me. We often wonder why the enemy seems to be constantly at our door, bringing problems and temptations. Could it possibly be because we are consistently providing food that attracts him? I assure you, the tarpon would not have been present if there was no food coming each day. Maybe you and I need to stop feeding the enemy of our lives by no longer feeding the old sin nature of our heart. The Spirit of God and the enemy of our souls do not feed on the same thing. If we have more activity in our life from the enemy than from the Spirit of God, try putting out a different kind of food. Try prayer instead of TV, Bible reading instead of questionable reading material, and fellowship with the people of God, not just those in the world. Stop feeding the enemy, and I assure you he will not be so quick to show up at your dock.

Matthew 6: 33, "But seek first His kingdom and His righteousness, and all these things will be given to you as well."

Know What the Printout Says

I recently took my boat in so the outboard engine could receive its three-year-service. When the service was completed and I picked up the boat, the dealership gave me a computer printout of how the engine had been run for the past three years. It showed how many hours it had been running and how long at different RPM's. It told me I had started the engine 950 times in three years.

What if the Holy Spirit did a printout of our lives at regular intervals? You know, with information like, "How long did we work for the Lord and how long for self?" Or maybe, "How much effort did we actually put into what we were doing, and what was our attitude"?

God does not have a printout like that, but He does know the thoughts and intents of our hearts. Even though there may not be a printout, He is aware of much more than we think. I appreciate knowing the statistics about my boat engine, because I depend on it to run properly when I am on the water. We should also appreciate the kind of information God seeks to show us about or own life and service for Him.

1 Corinthians 3:12-15, “If anyone builds on this foundation using gold, silver, costly stones, wood, hay or straw, their work will be shown for what it is, because the Day will bring it to light. It will be revealed with fire, and the fire will test the quality of each person’s work. If what has been built survives, the builder will receive a reward. If it is burned up, the builder will suffer loss, but yet will be saved, even though only as one escaping through the flames.”

When the Boat is Capsized

We were out for an afternoon boat ride when something caught our attention. Near some rocks, along the edge of a channel, we saw what turned out to be a capsized boat. It had apparently drifted upside down until it hit the shallow water, and was lodged there, bottom up. We looked around carefully, but never saw anyone nearby or in the water. I'm not sure what happened, but one thing is for sure, someone really had a bad day.

Sometimes life can hand us a bad day. You know the kind I mean...one that turns everything important to us upside down. We seem to just be drifting along with the current, not really knowing what may happen next.

You may be having one of those days, even while you read this. Can I tell you that you are not aimlessly drifting on life's current? Your life is being guided by the loving hands of a Savior who sees all, who is working everything for your good. He saw when your boat capsized, and He is ready to come to your rescue. All you need to do is take your eyes off what is going on around you, and begin to focus your faith and trust in Him. That's not always easy, but continuing to stay fixed on your capsized boat will not change the situation, it will only delay what God wants to do in your life. The Bible is not just some words in a book; it is the promise of a Savior who paid the ultimate price that you might belong to Him and Him alone. He can right any capsized situation in your life...if you will trust Him.

1Peter 5:7, "Casting all your care upon Him; for He cares for you. "

A Light Helps Find the Markers

It was to be a night fishing trip. We left the dock about 12:30 A.M., and began the slow ride down the canal to the river leading into the Gulf. I noticed the boat captain was not using a light, and asked how he would see the marker buoys? He said he did not have a spotlight. I "happened" to have one in my duffle bag, and quickly got it out and plugged it in. What a relief to be able to locate the marker buoys designating the channel we needed to follow. My relief quickly faded as the captain asked the question, "What side of the buoys should we be on?" I explained the green marker was to be on our right going out, and the red marker on our right when we returned. He didn't agree, and we almost ran aground twice before he began to follow my instructions.

Have you noticed how difficult it is to find the marker buoys in life without the light of the Holy Spirit to show you the way? God has a plan and purpose for your life, but, without the illumination of the Holy Spirit, we can still miss the way. Sad irony, even when someone tries to help us with truths from the Word of God, we sometimes still want to make our own choices. The man driving the boat that night was inexperienced, and, worse yet, slow to respond to help when it was offered. How about your life, and the choices you make? You cannot help being inexperienced, but refusing to acknowledge the help God sends is definitely a choice. We did get back in, but I really learned to be prepared.

Psalms 25:5, “Guide me in Your truth and teach me.”

Are the Stickers Consistent?

It was Labor Day, and I was out with my boys for a fishing trip. We were on the St. Johns River, near its mouth, heading to a favorite spot. As we ran along the center of the river, I looked to my left, and far over to the edge of the river, I saw a boat approaching with a blue light flashing. I slowed to a stop, and waited for the Marine Patrol to come alongside. The officer checked our equipment, our license, and then asked to see my boat registration. As I pulled it from my wallet, I panicked as I saw it went out of date August 31... it was now September 4. I told the officer it was out of date in August, "But I always purchase the registration, I just let it slip by." He was nice about it, and said, "I can see from the stickers you have placed one on top of the other you usually purchase the registration."

Thankfully, all I received was a warning.

When people view our lives, can they see consistent patterns in our habits that reflect who we are in Christ? We all make mistakes, but if our lives are consistent, and that consistency can be seen as we walk in Christ, people are more likely to be quick to forgive. I was grateful that day for the stickers I had placed one on top of the other.

Build consistent character every day in your life. When something happens, and you miss the mark, people will be quicker to understand that is not the real you. You are just having a bad day. Consistent character will define who we really are.

Hebrews 3:2, “He was faithful to the One who appointed him.”

Is Your Propeller Missing?

I started the engine and put the boat in gear, but nothing happened. I throttled up on the engine, but there was no movement of the boat at all. I put the boat in reverse, but same story. I asked my oldest son, Kenny, to go back and check the out-drive as I raised it out of the water. I asked him if there was anything wrong with the propeller. To my surprise, he said that there was "NO" propeller. Somehow, the retaining nut had worked loose, and the propeller was gone.

This can be a picture of our spiritual lives at times. All things seemed normal that day, until I tried to move the boat. Things can seem as usual to us spiritually, but when we are called upon to do something for the Lord, we find we have lost the faith that is needed to move us into obedience.

To the casual observer, all looked fine, but without that propeller, we were not going anywhere. We did not know anything was wrong, until we put the boat in gear. What would be the result of a call from God to your life today? Are you doing the things necessary to keep your faith and commitment strong in the Lord, or have you allowed the retaining nut that keeps your faith strong to work loose? I had another propeller that day, and after some ingenuity, we were able to get back in. Don't wait until the Lord speaks to your heart to discover you have allowed your faith and commitment to be lost. Check in often with God, so you will be ready to respond when He speaks to you.

Hebrews 11:6, "And without faith it is impossible to please God."

Don't Sweat the Messy Boat

We had planned a church fishing trip for the guys. It would be on January 1st. We would take two boats, and carry 11-12 men. The day dawned with perfect weather and an almost flat sea. The first stop began producing fish, and as both boats were close to each other, you can Imagine the chatter back and forth. It was the first time for several of the men, and you could see the excitement in their faces as fish after fish were coming aboard. The boats were soon a mess with blood and fish scales all over, but those catching the fish never seemed to notice, especially the new guys.

Many times, in our churches, there are problems and difficulties, but for those just coming in, getting saved, and developing a relationship with the Lord, they seem oblivious to it all. My son commented on the mess in his new boat as the day wore on, but one of the regulars just grabbed a bucket of water and splashed everything down. No reason to stop the fun, because some things were a little messy. Maybe we could adopt that attitude in the church. Just because things get a little messy, no need to panic and stop what the Lord wants to do.

We came back that day with 400 fish, eleven happy guys, and two very messy boats. The fellowship and great time was not ruined by the mess. The boats could be easily pressure washed. Don't let what appears to be a mess in the church get you down, God has a great pressure washer He is willing to use when it is necessary.

Psalms 51:7, "Cleanse me with hyssop, and I will be clean; wash me, and I will be whiter than snow."

Not Every Bump is a Real Fish

When I was still young, and not as smart as I hope I am today, two of my good friends and I were fishing under the Gandy Bridge on my boat. Fishing had been slow, and our young minds were looking for something to do. Several people were fishing off the catwalk on the bridge, and were unaware that we were just below them under the bridge. Young and mischievous, the three of us began to use our fishing rods to hit the lines of those on the bridge making them think they had a bite. We had to hold in the laughter, so they would not know what was happening.

The enemy is much like the three of us that day. He has all kinds of ways to simulate the reality of God, and if we are not careful, we will fall for it. How many times have we responded to what we thought was God, only to find ourselves going in the wrong direction? How many times have we made choices when we thought we heard from God, only to be seduced by the deception of the enemy?

For us, that day, it was just three guys playing pranks on some people who would not suffer any real harm. Unfortunately, the enemy never plays for fun, and making the wrong choices in this game of life can be disastrous. Don't allow the enemy to deceive you into making choices that can make a mess of your life. Next time you think you have a bite; you might want to make sure three crazy guys are not just slapping your line to make you think it is a fish.

John 10:27, "My sheep listen to my voice; I know them, and they follow me."

Some Things Attract Vultures

Fishing had been good, and, as usual, we had cleaned the many grunts we caught on the way in. We had also caught two nice grouper that I had to clean when I got home. Before cleaning the boat, I cleaned the two fish, and proceeded to throw the carcasses into the cypress bay head behind our house. The raccoons love me. I finished cleaning the boat, and went inside for a little rest. About an hour later, the neighbor next door rang the doorbell. When I answered, he asked, "Did you know there are at least a hundred vultures in the trees behind your house. OOPS!! My wife looked out in horror, and wanted to know what was going on. I did not realize that because of the water in the back, the carcasses of the fish would be floating and attract the vultures.

Have you noticed how sometimes the best laid plans can go wrong? It may even be something you have done previously, but this time there is a problem. In fact, what we do, without really considering the consequences, might actually be a means the enemy will use to attract the vultures in life. My plan seemed to be a good one, after all, the raccoons would love me. However, I never anticipated that the carcasses would attract such an audience. Sometimes, before we make what seems to be a perfectly good decision, we might want to check with the Lord to see if it will attract the wrong crowd, or result in something other than what we expect. The vultures are always lurking.

James 1:5, "If any of you lacks wisdom, you should ask God who gives generously to all without finding fault, and it will be given to you."

The Water is Not Always There

It was dark, and there was no moon, as we approached the small boat basin at Cedar Key. I backed the boat trailer down like so many times before, let the boat slide from the trailer, and parked the van. Three men and I got aboard and began to idle away from the dock, as we had on countless other occasions. Suddenly, the boat was stuck fast in mud, and the motor was kicking up muddy water. It was only then that I took out the spotlight to examine things around me. To my horror, the basin was all but void of water, and even the bridge we needed to go under had no water beneath it.

There are times in life that we find the same scenario played out. We have done the same thing so many times, that we fail to seek the wisdom and counsel of God. After all, I had done this many times; everything worked out fine when I did it before. What I had not anticipated that day was a strong East wind, aided by a full moon, had emptied the basin and now we were stuck.

The enemy is a master at playing to our comfort zone. He loves to get us so used to things that we fail to seek God, and never see the danger until it is too late. We were able to escape the basin that day, but that is a story for another time. Things are not always as they seem, or as they have been. Getting too comfortable is always a sure way to find yourself aground in your walk with God.

Proverbs 14:8, "The wisdom of the prudent is to understand his way, but the folly of fools is deceit."

Sometimes the Buoy Sinks

I had worked hard on the marker buoy I would use the next day to mark the precise spot where we would be fishing. I was actually proud of how it came out. As we approached the fishing spot where I wanted to drop the buoy, I took it from the locker, and dropped it over the side. The GPS said we were on the location. To my horror, the weight I had attached to the float to make it stand upright was too heavy, and I watched in shock as the buoy completely disappeared beneath the surface.

Sometimes, the effort we put into things in this life can just as quickly go south on us. We may have even prayed and sought the Lord concerning something. When it comes down to putting the buoy over the side, all the work and effort seems to disappear right before our eyes. During those times, we must be ready to look beyond our disappointments, and find the ever faithful hand of the Savior. The great reality of our relationship with Christ is that He will never fail. He will never leave us, nor forsake us. Even when it seems that what you have worked so hard to accomplish is falling apart, He remains faithful still.

Later in the day, we happened to hook the line on the buoy as we were fishing, and were able to retrieve it. I put a smaller piece of lead on it the next time. God is good, all the time, and all the time, God is good! The Lord seems to always have a way of working things out...maybe just not the way we had planned.

Luke 22:32, “But I have prayed for you, Simon, that your faith may not fail.”

Is The Plug in?

I launched the boat one day, looking forward to some fun with the family. I pulled the boat around, and put the nose up on the beach so I could go and park the van. When I returned to get in the boat, I was horrified to see that there were several inches of water in it. Of course, I knew immediately what had happened. I had forgotten to put the drain plug in before I launched the boat. Thank the Lord, I was able to get the plug in, and with the help of the bilge pump, remove the water from the boat.

Just as I needed the plug in the boat to keep the water of the lake from filling the boat, you and I must guard the doorway of our hearts to keep the things of this world from filling our life. For me that day, I was thankful for a good bilge pump to remove the water, and things were quickly back to normal. It is not quite that easy in life. The Holy Spirit can help us remove the unwanted things of this world, but the damage they have caused to us, and possibly our family, cannot always be reversed. The hurt in relationships, the loss of our testimony, the damage to our family, is not always erasable.

I can tell you that since that day, I have never left the plug out of the boat. Checking it, and making sure it is there, is a ritual in my preparations. I pray that will become true of my heart as well. Christian, are you checking the door of your heart regularly?

Proverbs 4:23, "Above all else, guard your heart, for everything you do flows from it.

Careful What You Lunge After

My friend, Ray, and I were fishing near the jetties on the St. Johns River on a pretty cold December day. We had already caught a couple of nice red fish, and I was tying the stringer on the back of the boat when it happened. I had placed my rod against the side of the boat while I retied the stringer, so I was not prepared when the fish hit. The rod quickly flipped overboard, and, by instinct, I lunged hard, trying to get it before it was out of reach. I suddenly found myself going over the side of the boat and into the chilly water. All thoughts of the rod were gone, and my concern turned to getting out of the cold water and back to the safety of the boat.

Things in life can also distract us and get our attention away from the important things, until it is too late. We can then make decisions out of anger, hurt, fear or anxiety, placing ourselves in a worse position than before. How many of us have reacted with our words to what someone said or did, and because we did not think it through, found ourselves floundering in a bad situation?

I did not get the rod back, but I learned a valuable lesson: Always place the rod in a rod holder, just in case. The same is true of our thoughts, of our actions, and, especially, our tongues. Life is full of surprises; it is critical that we place our words and actions in the care and safety of the Holy Spirit continually.

Psalms 19:14, "May the words of my mouth and the meditation of my heart be pleasing in your sight, Lord, my Rock and my Redeemer."

Is There Really No Hope?

I had sold the boat a few years before to a young man in our church. Now it was sitting in his yard, and I knew it had not been moved in a few months. I asked his dad about it, and was told the engine had a lower unit problem. I stopped by one day to look at it, and found it a foot deep in leaves and needing serious attention. I spoke to the young man, and found he wanted to sell it. I made him a low offer, based on the fact that he said it had a lower unit problem. He accepted my offer, and I took the boat home. I cleaned it up, put some gas in it, and found it started right up. I pulled the propeller to see if there was any obvious problem with the lower unit, and discovered the washer that held the prop at the proper place on the shaft was missing. I found a replacement washer, installed it, and realized there was nothing else wrong with the lower unit.

God is so good at doing the same thing with human beings. Sometimes we just give up on people. Sometimes lives seem so obviously broken, and the remedy to fix them appears to require more than we want to invest, or, at least, more than we feel capable of. Then God comes along, and with the work and wisdom of the Holy Spirit, He fixes the problem, and puts a life back together. The life that is seemingly in ruin just needs the repair work paid for by the work of Christ on the cross.

Matthew 11:28, "Come to me, all you who are weary and burdened, and I will give you rest."

Maybe the Wires Are Crossed

I had purchased a small Jon boat with the idea of using it to trout fish on the flats. The 20hp Mercury outboard looked very good, and the man said it worked fine. I paid him, and took my new prize home. When I put gas in the engine and pulled the cord, it backfired loudly, but did not start. I tried again with the same results. I pulled the cover off the engine, and while examining things under the cover, I noticed that the two sparkplug wires were reversed. I changed them, replaced the cover, and pulled the cord again. To my delight, the engine fired right up.

How easy it is to get the wires of our lives crossed up, whether in relationships, finances, or personal matters. When things aren't wired right in life, we can get a loud, and sometimes dangerous, backfire. Everything on the outside of the Mercury looked good, and gave no signs of needing any attention. I have no idea why someone reversed the wires; it was only when I tried to start it that the problem came to light. Our lives can be the same. For all those looking at us, we are the picture of what every person should be, but underneath, there is a real wiring problem.

Fixing what is wrong in your life may not be as easy as switching two wires was for me. There is a God, though, in Heaven that is a master mechanic. No matter what is wrong in your life, He can diagnose the problem and make whatever repairs are necessary.

Ephesians 3: 20, “Now to Him who is able to do immeasurably more than all we ask or imagine, according to His power that is at work within us.”

It’s Beneath the Green Mold?

As part of my love for fishing, I also have a love and appreciation for boats. No matter where I am, the sight of a boat will catch my attention. I can imagine what it would be like to be on them, moving across the water, and feeling the breeze in my face. I guess that's why I'm saddened when I see one that has been left neglected for a long period, not being used for what it was designed for. I drove by one recently that was a beautiful cabin cruiser, but had been setting so long that it was turning green with mold. Another one I noticed had grass a foot deep around it, so, likewise, it had not been used for a long time. How sad that something that was designed and constructed to bring so much fun, sits doing nothing, because the owner does not care, or does not have the time.

I wonder if that is how God feels when He sees our lives wasted on so many endeavors that have no real eternal value. The very thing we were designed and created for is put aside. We have become so caught up in other things, that we no longer use the gifts God gave us for His call on our lives.

I have bought a couple of boats like this, and have had a great time putting the fun back in them. God wants to do the same for our lives. He wants to put the value and usefulness back in the life that has been abandoned, broken, and allowed to be wasted.

Galatians 2:20b, “The life I now live in the body, I live by faith in the Son of God, who loved me and gave Himself for me.”

Just Know You Have a Fish

The clicker sounded on the large rod, and I reached over and pulled it from the rod holder. I reeled the line tight and set the hook. I knew from the resistance I felt that it was a very large fish. As I began to pull against the fish, I could not even move the line or pick up the rod tip. I was pulling on the 80 lb. test line as hard as I dared, but nothing was happening. There was no movement at all. One of the men on the boat with me remarked that I was probably just hung up on the bottom.

Have you ever gotten excited about something you felt God was doing in your life, or saying to you? Then someone, well intended or not, comes along, and says something intended to rob you of the excitement that you were feeling. The enemy will use any means to cause us to give up on what we believe God wants to do in our lives. He knows if he can get you to doubt what you feel God said, he can bring discouragement. He could ultimately cause you to give up on what God promised, or what you felt God wanted to do.

When you know you have heard from God, don't allow anyone, or anything, to convince you that you are just hung on the bottom. Always stay focused on what God has said, and allow Him to bring it to pass in your life.

The fish? It was a ten-foot nurse shark that weighed about four hundred pounds. I got it into the boat, so that I could touch it before letting it go.

Luke 21:33, "Heaven and earth will pass away, but my words will never pass away."

Are You Fishing or Sleeping?

Tim and I had decided to take a thirty-four-hour overnight fishing trip with a group of firemen. We would travel to the Florida middle grounds, about seventy to ninety miles west of Clearwater. It was a long trip for sure, but the fishing promised to be great. We left at 8:00 A.M., and began fishing around 1:00 P.M. that afternoon. All the guys were enjoying catching fish, and, before we knew it, it was close to midnight. That is when it happened. I noticed that many of the guys were sleeping in chairs, or finding a place to lie down and sleep. Are you kidding me? You paid good money to come to a great fishing area, the fish are biting, and you are sleeping the time away.

The same picture is seen among many who profess to have a relationship with Christ. We are living in a time when the need for the Gospel is greater than ever before. Men and women are struggling to understand the world around them, and, sad to say, many within the Church are not fishing, They are reclined somewhere, doing their own thing, or just plain sleeping. Jesus paid a huge price for the life we possess in Christ. He told us "...the harvest is white, but the 'fishermen' are few. Thank God someone was not sleeping when you and I needed to hear about Christ!

Ephesians 5:14-16, "Wake up, sleeper, rise from the dead, and Christ will shine on you. Be very careful, then, how you live - not as unwise, but as wise, making the most of every opportunity, because the days are evil."

Who Has the Steering?

My friend, Troy, had followed me out to the fishing area on his boat. It all started out well, but, shortly after arriving at the fishing area, the steering on his boat broke. The motor was running fine, but the steering wheel had no ability to move the engine, or control the direction of the boat.

I'm sure we have all met people a little like that, who seem to have it all together, but just do not seem to be able to steer their lives correctly. Great family, good job, many skills and talents, yet they just cannot seem to get it all together. Many times, these individuals are quick to blame everything and everyone. The reality is that they are unwilling to allow the Lord to provide the guidance they need. God is the only one who has insight into what is really going on, and when we refuse to listen, we are like Troy's boat, great power, but no control.

Does your life seem to be all mixed up and without direction? Are you having a difficult time navigating through the confusion and the obstacles of life? Maybe the real problem is that you are making the choices and decisions instead of leaving that up to God. Life can be difficult, but when you have learned to follow the directions of the Lord, when you have decided to allow Him to pilot your ship, He will always work things out for your best. He is not your co-pilot.

Isaiah 58:11, "The Lord will guide you always; He will satisfy your needs in a sun-scorched land, and will strengthen your frame. You will be like a well-watered garden, like a spring whose waters never fail."

Sharks Are Always on the Hunt

The day of fishing was ending, and I told the fellows to reel in the lines. It had been a great day, and everyone was tired and ready to go. I had a line out, and Dan asked if I wanted him to bring it in while I was busy with the boat. I said yes, and he began to reel the line in. To our surprise, the rod doubled over, and a fish was fighting against him. All of a sudden, it seemed the fish stopped fighting, and there was only dead weight on the line. When Dan got the fish in, we were all amazed to see what was left of a good sized red grouper. The back half had been taken off completely by a shark.

Have there been times in your life when what you were doing for the Lord was seemingly interrupted by something beyond your control? A missionary on the field is serving God when suddenly his wife is taken ill, and she passes away. A pastor's teenage son is arrested, and charged with a serious felony. A spouse tells you they do not love you anymore, and wants out. Life can suddenly interfere with what seems to be going so well, and we have no answers. This is when our real faith is tested. This is when what we are made of will really be determined. I cannot tell you why these things happen, but I can promise you that God is watching, and He is there to make sure that the outcome will achieve the best for your life.

Becoming the best that God has for you may not be easy; it may not even be what you would desire, but it will achieve His purpose and make you into His image.

Romans 8:28 is difficult to swallow sometimes, but it is God's great promise to those who will trust Him.

Check Your Bait Often

The fish were biting, and all the fellows in the boat with us were catching fish, except Mike. He had not gotten a bite for some time, but did not know what was wrong. He reeled in his line to see if there was a problem. He seemed somewhat surprised to find only a shiny hook, with no bait. Fishermen are always ready to share words of wisdom, so someone commented that no matter how hard he tried, he would not get a bite without some bait.

That is also true in our Christian life. Just to say we are Christians, or even to carry our Bible around with us, will not be enough to attract people to Christ. Every believer's life needs to be dressed with some bait. That bait may be words of encouragement, a willingness to listen when someone is hurting, or as simple as a hug at the right time. Of course, in fishing, the bait must target the fish you are trying to catch. In life, this is where the Holy Spirit comes in. He knows just what that person you are targeting for Christ needs. He can use the bait in your life, so that the love of Christ is obvious, because it is seen in you.

As you go about your day, make sure your life is displaying the right kind of bait to attract people to Christ. Just as a plain hook won't get it done in fishing, a life unconcerned about those around you will never attract anyone to the cross of Christ. Mike got his hook baited, and was back into catching the fish. Caught any fish lately? Check your bait.

Mark 1:17, "Come, follow me," Jesus said, "and I will send you out to fish for people."

Is Something Attached to You?

The young teenager with us reeled in the fish, but seemed surprised at what he saw on the end of the line. I told him it was a Remora, a fish with a suction area on the top of its head to attach itself to sharks. It does this to steal from the shark, and feed on the fish the shark has caught. I held the suction area to the young boy's hand, so the suction of the fish could be felt.

Just as the Remora is designed with the means of attaching itself to sharks, the enemy of our soul has ways of attaching his lies and deceptions to our minds. It may be in the form of guilt, bitterness, cynicism, or an array of other things. He will attempt to attach himself, and try to steal what God wants to do in our lives. It may even be in areas that seem harmless at first. As you try to accomplish what God has called you to do, you begin to find that something is always stealing the joy, peace, and victory that should be yours.

The shark has learned to accept the Remora as a part of its life. Many Christians have also given in, and just accepted the thing that is sucking the spiritual victory out of their lives. Are you finding it difficult to achieve victory in your Christian walk? Maybe a spiritual remora has attached itself to your life, and is stealing from you. Don't allow the remoras of the enemy rob you of what God wants to do in you and through you. You can defeat the thing that has attached itself to your life by surrendering it to Christ.

Galatians 5:1, "It is for freedom that Christ has set us free."

They Don't Belong in the Cooler

The rod tip was bending with the pull of the fish. The question was...what kind of fish? When it was brought into the boat, there was disappointment that it was only a lizard fish. This is labeled as a trash fish, because it is not considered by most to be good for eating. This is not what you are targeting to catch on your fishing trip.

There are also "trash fish" in every life that attempts to walk with Christ. These are things we encounter that take up our time and energy, but have little or no spiritual value. It is never the plan to come home with a cooler of trash fish. They are thrown back into the water, instead of taking up space in the cooler. Paul says our life can accumulate "wood, hay, and stubble," as we are serving the Lord, but these things will not pass the test; they are only spiritual "trash fish."

There are also "gold, silver, and precious stones,"... the groupers of life that have real value in our service for Christ. When it is time to stand before the Lord, and display our cooler of fish, we want to make sure it is not loaded with trash fish. In the fast-paced world we live in, we may be throwing the trash fish in the cooler. We allow them to take up the room that is needed for the grouper and other quality fish God is looking for. The trash fish may be fun to catch, but when it comes time to offer it to the Lord, make sure what you have in the cooler is worthwhile in His eyes.

1Corinthian 3:12-14, "If anyone builds on this foundation using gold, silver, or costly stones, the builder will receive a reward."

Swimming Free or Lead Bound?

The small grunt Kevin had caught was a perfect size to utilize as bait for the grouper we wanted to catch. We sometimes refer to this kind of bait as grouper candy, something a grouper cannot resist. I took the grunt, inserted the 9/0 circle hook carefully, and lowered it back over the side of the boat into the water. The poor grunt was probably grateful to be back in the water, as it immediately began to race for the bottom, some 40 feet away. The only problem, now he had a hook and line attached to him, and four ounces of lead that would restrict his movement. He probably knew immediately that his life was a target for every hungry fish in the water.

Have you ever felt like this poor grunt? You know the Lord, but there are things in your life that feel like the circle hook and the four ounces of lead that were attached to the grunt. You feel like no matter what you do, your life is always a target for every attack of the enemy that comes along. You just can't seem to get ahead, or win the battle.

Unlike the grunt, you have a promise from God, "I will never leave you, nor forsake you." This is not a promise that difficult things will not happen. When they do, God is right there with you, constantly fighting for you. The world may make you feel like this lowly grunt with the lead tied to it, but God's word is forever true in our life. You can swim the waters of life with confidence, because the God of the waters is on your side, and will fight on your behalf.

Isaiah 54:17, "No weapon forged against you will prevail."

When the Wake is Too Big

My dad and I were in Tampa Bay, fishing in the deep ship channel running toward the Skyway Bridge. Suddenly, my attention was drawn to a large ship that was coming up the channel. I told my dad that we needed to move a little ways from the channel until it passed. We pulled the anchor, and moved about two hundred feet away, and turned the bow of the boat to face the wake I knew was coming. As the first part of the wake reached us, I knew we were in trouble. The wake was over six feet high, and I could see the next one was even larger. The bow of the boat dipped hard, and struggled to rise quickly enough before the next wake.

Sometimes we make preparations for situations that are developing, believing that we know what is ahead, but find we are not even close. What we thought would be a small "wake" turns out to be a major disaster that places everything we are comfortable with in jeopardy. We can be grateful that the situation did not catch God by surprise, and He has a plan in place to bring us victory. We may not understand the reason for the trial, but we can trust God that He is in control. He will not allow the "wakes" of life to capsize us.

We survived the wake from the ship, and learned a valuable lesson in the process. We may not like the "wake" God is allowing to challenge our lives, but if we can learn from the experience, it is never wasted.

Psalms 34:4, "I sought the LORD, and He answered me; He delivered me from all my fears."

Don't Sweat the Scratches

I was proud of the new boat and motor I had just picked up from the dealer. I looked forward to trying it out as I drove to the Lowery Park boat ramp. I carefully launched the boat, and took extra care not to scratch the gold finish, as I left it tied up at the dock while parking the van. I was walking back to the dock when I saw the boat approaching. He was going much too fast, and I knew the wake he was putting out would slam my new boat very hard into the dock. I began running, but I knew I would not make it in time. I watched stunned as my new boat slammed into the dock, leaving a large gash in the shiny new finish.

Sadly, life can do the same thing to you and me at times. God has been wonderful, and we are feeling so blessed of the Lord in our walk and relationship with Him. Then, out of nowhere, someone or something slams our lives into the dock! There is a gash put in our lives that will be obvious to those around us. Maybe someone has done something to you that left a gash, with a failure on your part to respond appropriately. Perhaps you feel like your witness for Christ has been marred. God is a master at finding ways to heal and restore, even those who have been scarred in life. Yes, my new boat had a bad gash, but we used it many years, and, after a while, no one really noticed.

Jeremiah 18:4, "But the pot he was shaping from the clay was marred in his hands, so the potter formed it into another pot, shaping it as seemed best to him."

Can the Driver Really See?

It was going to be a great day. We were out on the boat with our youngest son, Danny, and his family, including young Darren and Timmy. Darren was only five, but he wanted to drive Granddaddy's boat. I sat him in the seat behind the steering wheel, but I realized he was not tall enough, so I kept my hand on it, also. I found I had to make adjustments for him, because he could not even see where he was going. He kept telling me, "I can do it," but I knew I could not take my hand off the wheel.

How many times have we wanted to steer our own lives, only to find the hand of God on the steering wheel. Like Darren, we might even feel that we don't need God's hand there, although we would not verbalize that thought. So often, we are making decisions, even when we cannot see beyond what is going on right now. We are blindly moving forward, not taking the time to seek for God's help and direction. If I had taken my hand off the wheel that day, Darren could have steered the boat, but I'm sure we would have run into something. God's love for us is what keeps His hand on the steering wheel of our lives. He knows we cannot see past the console, so He is keeping watch for us. When you and I learn to allow Him to steer the course of our lives, we will have reached a level of maturity that many never achieve.

Psalms 32:8, "I will instruct you and teach you in the way you should go; I will counsel you with my loving eye on you."

Know the Movement of the Tide

The sand bar north of Anclote Island is a wonderful place to park the boat, and spend some time walking the shoreline and picking up shells. There is just one note of warning that needs to be adhered to. Make sure that you are aware of whether the tide is moving in or out. One boat owner was obviously unaware of the value of that information. He apparently had parked the boat, and left to walk the sand bar, but while he was away, the tide went out, leaving the vessel high and dry. Now, he would have to wait for a few hours before the tide came back in, and he could move the stranded boat.

When you and I fail to understand the warfare we are in as we walk with Christ, we can also find our spiritual life high and dry. We can become so pre-occupied with life, that we forget that our spiritual vessel needs to be guarded, also. Just as neglecting to keep an eye on the tide resulted in the boat sitting on the beach, when we fail to spend the time we need in prayer, study of the Word, and fellowship with God's people, we will find our spiritual lives high and dry on the beach as well.

For the owner of the boat, it only meant waiting for the tide to return before he could get underway again, but spiritually, it could have far greater consequences. Maintaining our relationship with God is much easier than trying to get our lives off the beach once the tide has gone out and we are stranded.

1 Timothy 1:19, "Holding on to faith and a good conscience, which some have rejected, and so have suffered shipwreck with regard to the faith."

The Muck Can Bog You Down

We were excited to be with our youngest son, Danny, and the family, and ride the jet skis he had purchased. We eased out into the Anclote River to find an area where there was less boat traffic, and we could enjoy the ride. Everything was going well until Danny hit an area with his jet ski that was shallower than he expected. The grass on the bottom was clogging the water intake ports, and the craft could not get moving again. After several attempts to drive the jet ski out of the shallow area, it became apparent that the only option was to get off the jet ski and push it back to deeper water. Sounds easy enough until you step off the jet ski, and sink several inches into the muddy bottom of the shallow water. This was going to be a lot of work.

Life can often throw us the same kind of difficulty. We can make some poor decisions, and suddenly we are in very shallow spiritual water, unable to get our spiritual life moving again. It may even seem that when we try and push our way back to a place close to Christ, all we do is get bogged down in the muck and mire of the life around us. To the Church at Ephesus, Jesus said they had, "Left their first love." When life seems to get you bogged down and nothing seems to make much sense, go back to your first love. Allow your heart to once again experience that first love, a love that will never fail. Danny got back to deeper water, but the experience was one that he would not want to repeat.

Revelation 2:4, “Yet I hold this against you: You have forsaken the love you had at first.”

Maybe God Has a New Number

We left the dock at six, and headed into the darkness of the Gulf. About ten miles from shore, Cary looked at me. We both could smell the burning electrical wire, as Pete said that there was smoke coming from the back compartments. I quickly shut the engine down, and all the lights on the dash went out at the same time. Of all the times to not have a flashlight! I told the fellows with me that we would anchor the boat, and wait until there was enough light to see what the problem was. After dropping the anchor, I started pulling my rod down and getting ready to fish. I had no idea what was under the boat because the fish finder was out, but why just sit there worrying about something we could not control. Might as well fish!

Just because life throws us a bummer is no reason to sit, sulk, and complain. That attitude will accomplish nothing, and it could keep us from finding the blessing God has for us in the midst of the trouble. As we determine to "give thanks," we release the hand of God to begin to work in our circumstances. He can bring the blessings He has planned. As I dropped the bait to the bottom, I hooked up immediately, and within literally seconds, the other three fellows were hooked up as well. For almost an hour, we caught fish as fast as we could get the bait to the bottom. I fixed the wire and everything was back up and running again. We stopped and gave thanks to God for His safety and His bountiful blessings to us.

1Thessalonians 5:18, "Give thanks in all circumstances; for this is God's will for you in Christ Jesus."

Replace the Line and Fish

I saw the rod tip dip, and quickly reached to set the hook on the fish. I knew immediately that it was a very large fish, and the light rod and 30 lb. test line would have a tough time controlling it. All went well for a few minutes, as I was able to turn the fish each time it attempted to pull away from the boat. Suddenly, the fish turned, and began to move at a steady run away from the back of the boat. There was nothing I could do; even applying additional pressure to the spool with my thumb wasn't making any difference. I watched with dismay as the end of the line got closer and closer. Just before the fish emptied the reel on me, the line broke and the battle was over: fish one, Ken zero.

Maybe you've been engaged in a similar spiritual battle. You seem to be holding your own, then suddenly things take a radical turn and you realize things are making a run you will not be able to control. You do all the right things, but time and opportunity are running out, and you cannot do anything to stop the process. Life, like fishing, is not always fair, and you may not seem to be winning in every battle. Don't just focus on whatever it is you may have lost. Instead, focus on the fact that Jesus is faithful.

No, the end is not always determined by what "we" do. Sometimes, God has a plan that is different. If our hearts are only focused on the failures in life, we will miss all the wonderful experiences God brings to our lives and the blessing He has promised.

Psalms 111:7a, "The works of His hands are faithful and just."

Not Always as it Seems

I knew when I set the hook that it was a good fish. After a few minutes, I was excited to see the 24-inch Gag grouper at the surface. We placed it in the ice chest with the other fish we had caught. A few hours later, we were headed in and busy cleaning the fish. I told Cary I would give him one filet of the grouper, and removed the filet and put it in a bag. When I arrived home and told Susan about the grouper, she asked, "Did you get a picture?" I told her no, but I had only taken one filet off the fish, and the other side looked fine. I held up the good side of the half-cleaned fish for the picture, and was amazed to see you could not tell the other side of the fish was missing.

People's lives can be like that grouper. The side they show you looks wonderful, but the side they keep hidden is totally different.. the wife whose marriage is falling apart, the student who is being bullied at school, the senior whose health is fading...and they fear the worst. There are many lives in our churches, and in our neighborhoods, that are very different from what you see. God wants to make us sensitive to the needs of those around us, but we are so busy that we only see what we want to see, things which will not require much investment from us.

Maybe, today, we could look beyond the artificial smile on that person's face, and allow the Holy Spirit to show us where they are hurting, and how we could help.

1 John 3:16b, "And we ought to lay down our lives for our brothers and sisters."

The Officer Checks Everything

As the boat approached us, I somehow knew...as it got closer, I could see the two FWC officers in the boat and the blue light on the T-top. One officer asked if he could come on the boat. I said yes, and he proceeded to climb aboard. He checked our ID's, registration, life jackets, and several other things. He asked if we had caught any fish. I opened the ice chest, and showed him the grunts and one large gag grouper. He did not just want to see what I was showing him, but he wanted to check every compartment on the boat. He was unwilling to just skim over things.

I often feel that way when I am in prayer before the Lord. I may be there with my needs and petitions, but God seems to always be looking at everything. He opens first one door in my heart and then another.

I am glad we had nothing on the boat that day that we should not have had. However, I have been caught by God with things in my heart that should not have been there. If the officer had found something, it could have meant a fine, but, thankfully, He does not issue fines. He will, however, call us to give an account for what He finds.

I was confident the officer would find nothing amiss, because I am careful to follow the rules. I am also thankful that a loving, heavenly Father is teaching me to be even more careful with the contents of my heart.

Psalms 139:23-24, "Search me, God, and know my heart; test me and know my anxious thoughts. See if there is any offensive way in me, and lead me in the way everlasting."

Sharks Don't Belong in the Boat

The battle was on, and my brother, David, was pulling on the rod as hard as he could. In a few minutes, we could make out the large six-foot blacktip shark at the surface. As David kept the fish close in the water, we took some pictures, and I prepared to let it go. David then asked me if we could bring it into the boat for more pictures.

Over the years, I have watched people make that spiritual mistake in their life. They begin by flirting with things that they know could be dangerous in their lives, but the thrill, the excitement, the pleasure they feel seems to make the risk worth it, especially when their involvement is at a distance. Then it seems to always go further, as they begin to allow this new danger a place in their heart. It was not enough to just flirt with it at a distance, now they move to bring it into the boat of their heart, not fully aware of the consequences of what they are doing. The reality of the danger may not be obvious, until they have allowed the enemy to enter their heart and get a foothold that will be very difficult to dislodge.

A six-foot blacktip shark in the water is one thing, but that same six-foot shark in the confines of the boat can be very dangerous. Be careful what you flirt with in life. The enemy is never content with your flirtation with sin; he is seeking to convince you that you should bring the shark onto the boat. Do not let the excitement of the moment overrule your spiritual good sense.

Proverbs 4:23, "Above all else, guard your heart, for everything you do flows from it."

Don’t Keep a Short Fish

I could tell the fish Bill was fighting was a nice one. When he got it to the surface, a large cobia was on the line. I quickly netted the fish, and the question now was, "How big does it need to be to keep?" I told Bill I thought the size requirement was 28 inches to the fork of the tail. I was not positive, so I pulled out the latest FWC chart to make certain. To my surprise, the required size was 33 inches to the fork, longer than the fish Bill had caught.

I cannot tell you how many times as a pastor that I have been asked by an individual about something in his/her life that they were seeking to get approval for. I also cannot tell you how many times they had all their reasons for why they thought it was alright. When I would point out what the Scripture says, many times they would want to make excuses for why it was different in their case. Just as the FWC rule chart is the final word on the required size for fish, God's word is the final authority for our lives in Christ.

I am glad we did not try to fudge on the size of the fish. It was only a couple of hours later that the FWC boat came alongside to check what we had in the ice chest. We need to understand that God has rules for our lives to protect us...not to deny us the real pleasures of life. When we follow the rules in the scriptures, we never need to fear the presence of God making a visit to our heart.

1 John 1:9, “If we confess our sins, He is faithful and just and will forgive us our sins and purify us from all unrighteousness.”

Why am I Always Seasick?

Tracy loved to fish with us, but he really had a problem with seasickness. No matter how calm the water, he would be heaving over the side, sick within a few minutes of us stopping the boat. No matter what remedy he tried, it just didn't make any difference. He would still be chumming the water in a few minutes. Unfortunately, he would then begin to ask us to go back in. When you are several miles away from shore, that is just not something you can do, and it is not fair to the others on board. The day would then be spent watching him suffer with being seasick, and listening to the complaining because we would not go in.

Being around some Christians can be a lot like that. They are constantly suffering with things in their lives, because they refuse to listen to the Word of God and make better decisions. They struggle with finances, because they spend freely and don't bother to tithe. They deal with temptation, because they refuse to stay away from areas to which they are susceptible. They might struggle with addiction, because they will not take the necessary steps to be free. This is usually accompanied by complaint, and, even criticism, because the church, or other believers, are not doing their part to help. We need to ask God to help us take responsibility for our own actions and decisions, and learn to walk in obedience to His will.

We finally had to tell Tracy he could not go anymore. Unless we are willing to change, we may find our friend base dwindling, also.

James 1:22, "Do not merely listen to the Word, and so deceive yourselves. Do what it says."

Dark Clouds are a Warning

I had checked the weather radar before we left the dock, and knew there were storms about 50 to 70 miles offshore. I told the fellows we would watch the weather, and when we heard the first clap of thunder, we would head in. God blessed us with about five hours of fishing, and we continued to keep an eye on the dark weather heading our way. About noon, we heard our first rumblings of thunder off in the distance. The fish were still biting, but it was time to point the boat eastward and head in. As we followed the GPS back to the dock, we were amazed to see another boat coming our way, and eventually passing us

Being a pastor for 30 years, I can tell you I have seen my share of this kind of behavior in believers. It just doesn't seem to matter to them what the road ahead may hold; they are going that direction anyway. You can explain what the Word of God says, you can plead and beg, but they are going the way they want to go. They sometimes will even back up their decision by telling you God told them to do it. If you are going to make foolish decisions in life, you also need to be ready to accept responsibility for those decisions...not blame God, or anyone else, for the consequences.

I don't know what happened to the people on the boat that passed us, but I can tell you some stories of those who refused to listen to biblical wisdom concerning the wrong decisions they were making.

Proverbs 17:16, "Why should fools have money in hand to buy wisdom, when they are not able to understand it?"

It's Ok if the Trailer is Missing

My dad and I had enjoyed our time fishing and were back at the dock, ready to put the boat on the trailer and head home. We walked up to the truck and were shocked to find the toolbox had been broken into, and the trailer was gone. The boat was much too large and heavy to fit into the truck bed, so the only option was to find another trailer to use to get the boat home. I took the truck and went to the nearest pay phone (remember those days), and finally found a trailer I could rent for a twenty-four-hour period. We managed to get the boat on the trailer, and finally made it home.

You don't have to be a follower of Christ for long to find out that bad things can happen to good people. You can be doing all the right things, living for God the best you know how, and still find the trailer missing from the truck. One truth I have found is that no matter what the situation you have encountered, God has a plan and purpose for all of it. I may not recognize the plan and purpose, but if I trust God, and walk faithfully with Him, He will work it all out for my best.

I cannot tell you why God allowed our trailer to be stolen, but I can tell you that He was there to help us find a rental, the insurance replaced the trailer, and both my dad and I were no worse for the incident. The faithfulness of God never ceases to amaze me.

Romans 8:28, "And we know that in all things God works for the good of those who love Him, who have been called according to His purpose."

Know the Fish that Have Teeth

I have often watched as bass fishermen hold their catch by using their thumb and forefinger to grip the lower lip of the fish, effectively causing the fish to be ridged and unable to move. Because I usually fish in salt water, I know that is not a good method when holding saltwater fish. Most saltwater fish have very sharp teeth, and placing a finger in their mouth is inviting disaster.

We can make the same mistake when we are dealing with many of the issues we are faced with in life. Being unaware of all the facts can cause us to say or do things that can be painful, not only to ourselves, but to others, also.

Handling a fish properly, so that you do not injure yourself, requires us to be aware of the dangers that are present. Handling some of the situations we are confronted with in life also requires that we be aware of the dangers that may be present. After your thumb is cut and bleeding is too late to notice that the speckled trout has some vicious teeth in its mouth. The same is true in life. Being oblivious to the dangers in our spiritual decisions is a poor excuse. We need to learn to approach those situations in our lives that are often froth with danger, being guided and directed by the Holy Spirit. There is never a guarantee that you will not be hurt, disappointed, or deceived, but when we are allowing the Holy Spirit to guide us, we can be assured that He has every situation under His control.

James 1:5, "If any of you lacks wisdom, you should ask God, who gives generously to all without finding fault, and it will be given to you."

Those Sand Granules Can Hurt

Lenny asked me to go shrimping with him on his bass boat. The boat had a 150 HP motor, and would run over 60 mph. I stepped on the boat from the beach that morning, not thinking about the sand I deposited on the carpet from the bottom of my shoes. We eased away from the shore, and Lenny shoved the throttle forward until we were flying across the water. It was then that I was reminded of the sand I had deposited on the carpet, as it was now flying in my face at over 50 mph. It felt like small BB pellets fired from a gun as it struck my skin. What had seemed fairly insignificant, only a few minutes before, was totally different now.

How true this can be in our day-to-day life. The choices and decisions we are making at the moment may not even catch our attention, but, later, because of a change in our circumstances, those decisions can really hurt. The Christian life is all about how we make choices and decisions. When what we do or say, how we treat others, or the thoughts allowed in our mind are not under the direction and control of the Holy Spirit, they can come back to bite us later. Those areas of our lives that may seem to be hidden from view, and unnoticed by most, can come to light at the most awkward times.

Make your decisions and choices carefully, under the leading of the Holy Spirit. You may run into them again, and the pain could be significant. Words or actions that have come in haste can be disastrous later.

Philippians 2:5, "Let this mind be in you, which was also in Christ Jesus."

We Are Better Together

I was fishing beneath one of the bridges in Tampa Bay with Susan's dad, and, Otts, his father-in-law. Otts was up in years and had some heart issues, but was having a great time. Suddenly, the drag began to scream on the large spinning rod, so I quickly set the hook and handed the rod to Otts. He fought determinedly, but the fish was getting the upper hand. Without warning, Otts suddenly handed me the rod and told me he couldn't fight the fish any longer. The look on his face told me he was exhausted, so I took the rod and continued the fight. I was younger and had more strength, so I was able to get the fish to the boat. It had taken a joint effort, but the conclusion was worth it.

How many times have we seen God use the gifts and talents of more than one individual to get a job done? Sometimes one individual seems to reach the limit of what they can do, but they are willing to allow someone else to step up and help them. There are also those with the "Lone Ranger" attitude, and the work God wanted to accomplish does not get completed because that person was unwilling to receive help.

The body of Christ has been blessed with a variety of people and many talents. When we are willing to allow others to join us in a vision or purpose, God is pleased with His body. Are you doing something that seems more than you can handle? Seek others who are willing to come alongside and lend a hand. It could mean the difference between success and failure.

Ecclesiastes 4:9, “Two are better than one, because they have a good return for their labor.”

The Reward May be in the Attic

For several years, Susan's dad lived near the original Bass Pro store in Springfield, Missouri. Over the years, his love for fishing had seen his stock of fishing tackle and accessories increase to a pretty substantial level. One year, as Susan and I were planning our trip to see them, he called, and asked me to bring the van. That was a little unusual, but I said sure. One morning, while we were there, he told me to follow him to the garage. He began to pull all the fishing stuff he had accumulated out of the attic, and told me it was all mine now. I protested "mildly," but he assured me that he wanted me to have it. He finished in the attic, then pointed to the corner of the garage, and said, "Take that, too." Now I was really surprised, because in the corner on a stand was an almost new 20 hp Mercury outboard. I was certainly glad I had been willing to bring the van as he had asked.

I wish I was always as quick to be obedient to the voice of the Lord. Many times God will ask us to do something, maybe even something that doesn't make sense, and we are slow to respond. No matter what God asks of us, He always has something in mind that will bless us, and has designed every effort we make to be worthwhile.

The next time the heavenly Father asks you to do something that you would rather not do, remember God has a huge attic, and always wants to bless you with some of His stuff.

Deuteronomy 28:2, “And all these blessings shall come on thee, and overtake thee, if thou shalt hearken unto the voice of the LORD thy God.”

The Weather Changes the Game

It was my first time to fish in a kayak, but I was looking forward to fishing with Cary, and learning something new. I was familiar with the sound of a motor on the back, so it took a while to get used to the fact that, unless you paddled, the kayak did not move, and even then, it was not fast. We fished a couple of hours, but then began to notice the weather changing just offshore. The sky was dark and we could feel the wind picking up, and we were still some distance from the dock. We turned the kayak around, and we both began to paddle, as we headed for the safety of the boat ramp. We got to the ramp just as the heavy winds hit, but were amazed to see a man in a small Jon boat leaving the dock. What was he thinking, or was he even thinking?

In our spiritual life, we will often come up against some real situations where the enemy wants to destroy us. When we begin to see what is happening, we need to remember that our safe harbor is found in our relationship with Jesus Christ. We must place our lives in His hands if we expect to ride out the approaching storm. Don't be like the man who was leaving the dock, but recognize that you are no match for the enemy on his turf. Don't trust your own skills, but put your trust in the One who loves you.

The man quickly saw how foolish it was to leave the shore and came back. It's never too late to recognize the foolishness of a decision we made, and call out to a loving heavenly Father.

Proverbs 2:8, "He guards the course of the just, and protects the way of His faithful ones."

Is a Course Change Needed?

The Lowrance GPS unit I have has a great feature. It draws a "bread crumb" trail, a series of dots, from my present location, to where I want to go. All I need to do is keep the curser on the dotted line to get to my destination. The problem comes when there is a crab trap buoy, a boat, or, at times, a shallow place or even a body of land in the path the GPS has laid out. As the driver of the boat, I must maneuver the boat around these obstacles, and then back on course again.

In our spiritual lives, God has a divine line drawn from where we are to where He has planned for us to go. The difficulty comes as the enemy places obstacles in our path. They may be as small as the crab trap buoy, that takes only a slight maneuver to dodge them, or they may seem as large as an island when first encountered.

While the boat's GPS may not make allowances for these obstacles, the Holy Spirit that guides your life certainly does. What seems to be an obstacle, taking us from the course God has for our life, can actually prove to be vitally necessary for us to become all God has planned for our lives. The important thing is that the God, who charted the path for your life, is not caught off guard by the obstacles you encounter. He will give you the strength to maneuver around them and return to the desired course, if you will just trust Him.

Proverbs 3:5-6, "Trust in the Lord with all your heart, and lean not unto your own understanding. In all thy ways acknowledge Him, and He shall direct thy paths."

Watch for the Old Sweatshirts

Our good friends, Don and Doris, were with Susan and me, as we headed out the small river toward the flats on the edge of the Gulf. We were in unfamiliar water, so I let the boat idle along slowly. Suddenly, there was a violent vibration in the boats out-drive, and the boat was struggling to move forward. I pressed the trim button to lift the out-drive, so I could see what might be wrong. I found that an old sweatshirt that had been discarded in the water was wrapped tightly around the propeller. I pulled out my knife, knowing that removing the sweatshirt would require some effort.

Believe it or not, life can often wrap an old sweatshirt around our spiritual life, bringing with it violent shaking, and seemingly bringing our life to a standstill. The marriage you thought would last forever is over with the signing of a document. The pregnancy you had prayed for ends early, as the doctor tells you there is no heartbeat. The job you thought would be your lifelong career downsizes you off the payroll. It is not your fault, nor can you understand why God would allow this to happen to you.

Truthfully, I cannot answer those questions, but I can point you to a loving heavenly Father that will help you cut and tear away that old sweatshirt that is trying to destroy your life. With His love, guidance, and support, you can get under way again. Old sweatshirts can show up in totally unexpected places, and in a variety of ways, but God's love for us is constant, sure, and sufficient.

Psalms 121:7-8, “The Lord will keep you from all harm. He will watch over your life; the Lord will watch over your coming and going both now and forevermore.”

I Need All Cylinders Working

I had owned the outboard for several years, and it had always run flawlessly. As we were running out to our fishing spot, I detected something was wrong with the engine and throttled it back to an idle. It shut down, and as hard as we tried, it would not restart. For nearly two hours, we worked at getting the engine started. Suddenly, it fired up, and we began quickly heading back to the dock. When I had the engine checked later, they discovered that one of the four pistons had a hole in the top. You would think that if the other three were working, it should not be such a problem.

We sometimes feel the same way about our spiritual life. As long as we do more good than bad, as long as we only make wrong choices occasionally, then things should be fine. This one small sin God surely understands, and, after all, there are plenty of other people doing the same thing and they seem to be getting along fine.

We were fortunate to get the motor running again that day, and get back to the dock. The engine was never designed to run on three pistons instead of four. Our lives are not designed to function in slight disobedience to God's Word. Before the engine could be fully trusted again, I had to replace the burned piston. Before your life will be all God has in mind, you need to repent and move in the direction of obedience to the Lord. Continued disobedience will ultimately cause a breakdown in your relationship with Christ. Your relationship with Him will not be whole.

Hebrews 12:1, "Let us throw off everything that hinders and the sin that so easily entangles."

More Than a Sunken Hull

My eye caught the Glastron boat that was for sale. I knew the man who owned it, and soon found that he was selling it because it had sank at the dock and would not start. What he was asking for it told me he did not feel the boat would ever be worth anything. Always looking for a challenge, I purchased the outfit and took it home. My son, Kenny, and I got the engine to turn over, and when I put some gas in the carburetors, it fired right up. After some work on the floor, a little on the transom, a new paint job, new seats and carpet, the boat was a real beauty. You can imagine how I felt the first day as I hooked it to my truck, and put it in the water. Soon, I was flying across the lake.

There is something about taking an item, that others see as having little or no value, and, with some time, and investment of money, making something special. We can see that played out day after day within the Kingdom of God. Our lives have been submerged in sin and the consequences of that sin, and do not seem to possess any obvious value. It was in our despair and brokenness that Jesus found us. Always looking for a challenge, He took and invested Himself in each of our lives. There was a high cost, and it took some time and a lot of love on the part of Christ, but the finished product looked brand new.

No matter what your life looks like, Christ is always looking for a challenge.

2 Corinthians 5:17, "Therefore if any man be in Christ, he is a new creature: old things are passed away; behold all things are become new."

Sore and Tired is No Excuse

As fast as we put the bait in the water, we were set up on another fish...sometimes two on the double hook rig we were using. Jim had landed his share, and he began to express the pain he was feeling in his forearm. Finally, he put the rod down, and blurted out, "That's it for me, I can't fight another fish". We continued to pull in fish, and in a few minutes, Jim picked up his rod again, and said, "I can't stand this," and he began fishing again.

Sometimes the work we are doing for the Lord seems to become too much for us, even though it was exciting in the beginning. The problems and difficulties we face seem to rob us of our strength, energy, and even our desire to continue. We may even experience pain, as a result of our work for Christ.

Jeremiah knew how this felt. It seemed like the entire nation of Israel was against him, and even God expected more than Jeremiah could give. In times like these, we may feel like quitting. Thank God for His Holy Spirit within us, and it is in our weakness that His strength is seen. Quitting may seem to be what you need to do. If the Holy Spirit has really called you to your task, you will not be able to step away for very long. Just as Jim had to pick up the fishing rod again, and Jeremiah had to continue to speak the word, the Holy Spirit will give you the strength to continue your work for Christ.

Jeremiah 20:9, "His word is in my heart like a fire, a fire shut up in my bones. I am weary of holding it in; I cannot do it any longer."

Know When It's Out of Season

The fish was going to meet the size limit for sure, but was it a gag grouper that was out of season, or a red grouper that we could put in the cooler? As the color soon became visible, I was disappointed to see that it was a large gag grouper, large enough at over 24 inches, but the wrong species. The season was closed for this fish, so he would have to go back for another day. Keeping the fish was not an option...the fine was much too high, and, more important, God holds us to a greater standard.

How many times have we faced, in our walk with God, a similar situation in our personal life? Something comes up, or we receive an offer that really looks and sounds good. That still small voice within our heart says, "Put it back in the water; it's not in season for you." If we are not careful, the natural man attempts to rationalize, and try to justify why it is not really wrong. In spite of God's warning, we may even consider putting that thing in the cooler of our lives.

Sometimes things that come along in our lives are not wrong, they are just not the best for us right now. No matter how good it may seem to you, if God says it is "Out of Season," let it slide out of your hands and back into the water. There may be a day that God will allow it for your life, but that day is just not today. God is the only one Who knows the future, and what is in season as truly best for our life.

Ecclesiastes 3:1, "There is a time for everything, and a season for every activity under the heavens."

Look Beyond the Outward

I could tell the 20' Welcraft boat had been setting there for several years. All four tires were flat and dry rotted, the hull was green from the mold growing on it, and the weeds were growing inside the boat as well as outside. I could only guess why the owner had allowed it to get in such bad shape. I was looking beyond the surface, and, to me, it was a chance to have the offshore boat I had always dreamed of. It would require a lot of work, but I knew I could do most of it myself, and working for a dream is not really like work anyway. I purchased the boat "dirt cheap," no pun intended, and spent the next several weeks getting it into shape for its maiden voyage on the Gulf.

The way I felt, as I surveyed the possibilities of that boat, is perhaps how God must feel as He looks at all the broken and wasted lives that He has purchased. While many people drove by, never giving a second thought to the possibilities in that boat, I saw something completely different. That certainly is true as God surveys our lives. While many may pass by and see nothing of value, God sees the potential that is hiding just beneath the wasted years, the obvious scars and pain, and the sin that seems to be flourishing everywhere.

No matter what shape God may find us in, He is ready to invest whatever is necessary, so that we can reach our potential in Christ. What does God see in your life that He is ready to claim for His Kingdom?

2 Corinthians 5:17, "Therefore, if anyone is in Christ, the new creation has come: The old has gone, the new is here!"

The Fog Can be Blinding

The day offshore had been great, and the weather was beautiful. As I pointed the bow of the boat eastward, off in the distance there seemed to be a haze over the water. As we got closer, the haze turned out to be a dense sea fog. We entered the fog bank, and slowed down. It was obvious that I would need to follow the GPS and compass closely. The fog was so dense, we could barely see thirty yards in any direction, and the exact location of the sun could not even be determined.

Life can often throw us a similar problem. One minute things seem to be going great, life could not be any better, and, all of a sudden, everything rapidly goes south on you. The plan and direction for your life was clear, now, not only are you not sure of what to do, you can't even discern the voice of the Holy Spirit. To make matters worse, there does not even seem to be a light at the end of the tunnel.

Just as I had to trust the accuracy of the compass and GPS that day, you and I, as followers of Christ, have to trust the truth and accuracy of God's Word. In those times, when there seems to be no answer to what we have encountered, the Word of God is the sure compass we can depend on. His Word is faithful when all else seems to have abandoned us. Follow the guidance that is found in the Word. You will exit the fog, just as we did that day with the channel marker we were looking for right in front of us.

Ps 119:105, "Your word is a lamp for my feet, a light on my path."

You Need Some Extra Pull

We were planning to move to the next fishing spot, but when Brandon tried to retrieve the anchor, it was hung fast on the rocks below. No matter how hard he pulled, he could not dislodge the anchor. He looked at me to see if there was anything at all that we could do. I told him to wrap the rope securely around the bow cleat, and hold onto the rope tightly. I put the 250 HP outboard in gear, and it pushed the 3500-pound boat forward, easily pulling the anchor from the rocks. All the best efforts that Brandon could put forth did not compare to the combined strength of the boat and its motor.

Many times, we get our lives hung up on the rocks of this world. No matter what we try, attempting to break free, we come up defeated in trying to dislodge the hold on our lives. Freedom from the bondages of this world is only possible, as we fully submit our lives to the Lord Jesus Christ. Allow the Holy Spirit to use the Word of God to pull you free from that bondage. In our own strength, we are no match for the strongholds and addictions we encounter in this life. We are no match for the hurts and pains that can grip our lives. They refuse all our efforts to pull free.

Let me encourage you to wrap your life around the Word of God. Allow the Holy Spirit to empower that Word to quicken your heart; and watch what that combination can do to bring freedom in your life!

2 Corinthians 10:4, "The weapons we fight with are not the weapons of the world. On the contrary, they have divine power to demolish strongholds."

It Will Bend Back Again

Because I am often fishing over rock and structure, I found that a grappling hook anchor holds the boat firmly in place. The problem comes when it gets hung on the rocks, and I have to use the weight of the boat and the power of the engine to pull it loose. When it comes loose, and we pull it to the surface, there are always one or two of the stainless steel prongs that no longer have the correct bend in them. Because the stainless steel is somewhat softer than regular steel, its flexibility allows me to put a pipe over the prong, and bend it back to the desired shape without it breaking. Over the years using the anchor, I have bent the prongs back into shape many times.

Thank God, He has created you and me with a great deal of flexibility. The enemy can put us in bondage, and gaining our freedom may leave us somewhat bent to the wrong shape. Like the anchor, God can use the Holy Spirit to put us back as we need to be. Life can be unfair. Our failure in temptation, or the brokenness we may be feeling from a bad relationship, seems to have bent us beyond repair or usefulness. The enemy tells us lies, and says that things will never be the same. God speaks, and tells us that if we will allow Him to impart the Holy Spirit into our lives, that we can be even better than new. Choose to believe what God has promised, because He will not fail.

2 Corinthians 10:5, "We demolish arguments and every pretension that sets itself up against the knowledge of God, and we take captive every thought to make it obedient to Christ."

There's a Reason for a Leader

When a fisherman prepares his fishing tackle, one of the critical parts of the rig is the leader. The leader is the last section of line, or wire, just before the hook. The leader is usually heavier than the other part of the line. It is designed to take the added stress and abuse from coming in contact with the fish, or the structure that is encountered as the fish is fighting. It is important that the fisherman keeps a close watch on the condition of the leader, or he could lose a trophy fish because of the wear on this important part.

In your life, and mine, God wants the Holy Spirit to be the leader. He wants the Holy Spirit to be the one who takes the lumps, bruises, sharp obstacles, and abrasions that will invariably come our way. The enemy is constantly trying to drag us through every problem and bad situation he can, in order to kill, steal, and destroy our lives and our relationship with Christ. Unfortunately, we often want to take the lead in our lives. We have that urge to be in control, not understanding that when we are in the lead, we often suffer things that God never intended for us. Allow the Holy Spirit to be the leader in your life. Allow Him to run that interference that is necessary to keep you safe and committed to Christ. Just as the leader on the fishing line can make the difference in victory or defeat, allowing the Holy Spirit to lead in our lives will always bring the victory we need.

John 14:16, "And I will ask the Father, and He will give you another advocate to help you and be with you forever."

Be Prepared to Set the Hook

I controlled the spool of the reel with my thumb, as the bait and four ounces of lead raced to the bottom. When the lead hit bottom, I pushed the button on the clicker, left the reel in free spool, and waited for the sound that would tell me a fish had hit. It only took a minute before the clicker began to sing, and I reached for the rod to set the hook. I jerked the rod as hard as I could, but felt no resistance. I had forgotten to take the reel out of free spool, and engage the drive to the handle! I lost the fish.

The same can be true, as we are attempting to bring someone to Christ. No matter how much we have invested in telling them about Jesus, if we are not spiritually ready when prompted by the Holy Spirit, the appropriate time can be lost. Only God knows the best time and place to reach a person for the Lord. We need to do more than just listen for the voice of the Holy Spirit. We need to be ready ourselves to act when He speaks. We cannot allow the distractions of the world, or the temptations of the enemy, to cause us to be unprepared to pray with someone when the Holy Spirit prompts us.

I heard the clicker clearly, but forgetting to engage the reel spool gave the fish all the advantage and the time it needed to get away. That perfect opportunity may never come again. Don't allow a soul to miss the Kingdom of God...be ready to strike at a moment's notice by staying prepared.

2 Corinthians 6:2b, “I tell you, now is the time of God's favor, now is the day of salvation.”

The Swivel Prevents Line Twist

For those who may be unfamiliar with the terminology, a swivel on a fishing line allows the fish or bait to twist and turn, without placing a dangerous twist or kink in the main line. The line from the reel and the line from the hook are fastened to opposite ends of the swivel, so they can turn independently of each other. The line can twist, and become a nightmare to untangle, without the swivel working properly.

Thank God, He has supplied believers with a spiritual swivel in our lives. Scripture declares that, "We are in the world, but not of the world." No matter what is going on around us in the world, we need not be moved by it, or get entangled by it in our spiritual life. The Holy Spirit within us acts like a spiritual swivel, allowing us to be used by God to minister to this world. It prevents the world from wrecking and ruining our walk with Christ. Jesus knew we would need to be close to those who are in the world, but He also knew that the enemy would be constantly trying to trap us and drag us down. Thus, the Holy Spirit lives in our lives, so we can be "in the world, but not of the world."

A fisherman will sometimes be in a hurry, and tie the hook directly to his line, but it will ultimately cost him more time trying to get the twist undone. As a child of God, don't try to cut corners...allow the Holy Spirit to be the spiritual swivel in your life, and keep the twist out!

John17:16, “They are not of the world, even as I am not of it.”

Keep Your Hands off the Drag

I knew when Jim set the hook that the fish was big. I knew he would need to keep the fish out of the structure below, if he was to have a chance of landing it. As I heard the drag giving line, I was afraid the fish was winning the battle, so I reached over and tightened the drag to put more pressure on the fish. Suddenly, the bend in the rod was gone and the line slack. In my effort to help Jim with the fish, I had over tightened the drag, and the fish had broken off.

We live in a day of many changes within the church. Young believers are trying to find their place in God's plan and purpose. Many of us, who are older, are too quick to make a judgment of what is going on, and if it will work. We want to reach over, and tighten the drag on their spiritual lives. In the process, we not only can impede their growth in Christ, but we have often driven them from the church and God's desire for their lives. We need to allow the Holy Spirit to be the One that is in control of the drag and set the standards in for them. He knows how to guide their choices without endangering the potential they have for Christ.

Would Jim have been able to land the fish without my interference? Who knows? I am sure my decision to tighten the drag proved disastrous that day. Let's cheer this new generation on without being so quick to tighten the drag in their spiritual lives.

Romans 14:4, "Who are you to judge someone else's servant? To their own master, servants stand or fall. And they will stand, for the Lord is able to make them stand."

Ordinary to Extraordinary

Cary, a close friend of mine had purchased a very nice Kayak, so he could fish the inshore areas. Before long, he was telling me and showing me, all the alterations he had made that would allow him better use of it. I was amazed at his work and effort that made what had been just a regular kayak into a real inshore fishing machine. He had added two trolling motors and an attachment that allowed him to stand and fish.

God works the same way in your life and mine. We were just ordinary people, or maybe even less than ordinary, when He found and purchased us. Instead of being satisfied with leaving us as we were, He began to make the alterations necessary in our lives, so we would be all He wanted us to be. Because of His work in us, what was once ordinary, or less, has now become extraordinary. A life that had no purpose, had little real value, and was heading nowhere in particular, has become a powerful man or woman of God.

God is still in the business of taking ordinary lives, and transforming them by the power of Jesus Christ. God sees the potential in you, and is willing to make all the alterations necessary to achieve His purpose for your life. My friend went from having just an ordinary kayak that few people noticed, to possessing a real inshore fishing machine that turns heads whenever he is out in it. God does the same in our lives.

Galatians 2:20, "I have been crucified with Christ and I no longer live, but Christ lives in me. The life I now live in the body, I live by faith in the Son of God, who loved me and gave Himself for me."

Not all Hulls are Alike

I love to go to boat shows, and see all the different styles of boats. One difference is the design of the hull. There are four basic designs to the powerboat hull: the flat bottom, the semi-vee, the deep-vee, and the catamaran, or twin-vee hull. Each has a different use, and is very effective when used as they were designed. The flat bottom hull will run in very shallow water, but is not practical in rough choppy water. The semi-vee can run in somewhat shallow, and can also handle a moderate chop. The deep-vee does not do as well in shallow water, but provides a much better ride in the rough offshore seas. The catamaran, or twin-vee, will ride very well in rough water, but the handling in turns can be a little tricky if you are not used to it.

As I have followed Christ, I find Christians are as varied as boat hulls. Some believers do very well, as long as the doctrine is shallow, and there are minor waves in their lives. There are also believers who have a little more depth in their knowledge, and can brave a little more roughness in life. You also have the believer who has been diligent in their study of the Word, they have applied the truth of that word affectively to their life, and they can handle most of what life throws their way. You also have those with a twin-vee hull who can have a solid foundation, but they can be a little tricky to handle sometimes. We all have a place in the Church, and the Holy Spirit knows how to best use us.

1Corinthians 12:27, “Now you are the body of Christ, and each one of you is a part of it.”

Just Noise if Out of the Water

We were ready to move to another spot, so I put the engine in gear and shoved the throttle forward. The engine revved quickly, and the loud splash of water told me the trim on the engine was much too high, putting the propeller out of the water. I pulled the throttle back, lowered the trim on the engine, and, once again, put the engine into gear. This time the response was quick and effective.

The problem that I experienced that day was easy to remedy, but there are those in the church experiencing the same kind of spiritual problem, but can't seem to find the right solution. All I needed to do was make sure the propeller was completely immersed in the water, before I tried to accelerate or move forward. In reality, that is the solution for many who find their life in Christ may make a lot of noise, but doesn't seem to get them very far. Trying to do the work of Christ without your life being completely immersed in His love, may create a lot of noise and activity, but will have no real positive affect on people's lives.

If you continue to run the outboard propeller out of the water, something can be damaged. Continuing to move in the Kingdom without love will also create damage in the lives you are trying to influence.

1Corinthians 13:1-2, "If I speak in the tongues of men or of angels, but do not have love, I am only a resounding gong or a clanging cymbal. If I have the gift of prophecy and can fathom all mysteries and all knowledge, and if I have a faith that can move mountains, but do not have love, I am nothing."

The Value of the Level Wind

One invention found on bait casting reels has been a tremendous help to those who use them. It is called a level wind mechanism. It moves the line back and forth over the spool as the line is retrieved, allowing the line to fill the spool evenly. This prevents the line from building up in a single area of the spool, which would cause the spool to jam or tangle.

Unfortunately, many Christians do not have an affective level wind mechanism in their spiritual life. Instead of allowing the Holy Spirit to grow them in a level and balanced manor, they often become dogmatic, or legalistic, in one or more areas. This unnatural focus on a singular ideology becomes destructive to their potential for Christ, and often wrecks the relationships they need in life. This buildup in one area often causes them to be critical of the church, ministries that they do not agree with, and causes them to isolate themselves from brothers and sisters in Christ. They develop a mindset that they are the only ones who have the true spiritual understanding of what it means to be a Christian.

We need to allow the Holy Spirit to be the level wind mechanism in our lives, and help us to grow evenly in our understanding of God's word. Just as a reel without a level wind stands the chance of becoming jammed or tangled, so do those who get so focused on a single area of doctrine that they miss the real value of Scripture.

2 Timothy 2:15, "Do your best to present yourself to God as one approved, a worker who does not need to be ashamed, and who correctly handles the word of truth."

Better to Listen to the Captain

There would be almost a hundred of us on the large head boat. We were going offshore for a nine-hour fishing trip. As the boat pulled away from the dock, the captain's voice came across the speakers, and he proceeded to give us instructions for the day of fishing. There were some safety instructions, but he also let us know the things we could and could not do while on the boat. There were even instructions for when we could let our lines down, and when to pick them up. Those of us on the boat that day listened intently, and tried to follow the instructions given them by an individual they did not even know. They were placing their success in fishing, and even their safety, in the hands of a man they had never met.

How ironic that we can do that in so many different situations in life, and find it difficult to do the same when it comes to our heavenly Father. God gives us His safety instructions, guidance for life, and promises that all He allows in our lives will bring us success. Those who comply with the boat captain's directions can have an enjoyable day of fishing. Those who learn to comply with God's manual of instructions, the Bible, will also find that life can be lived to the full.

Not one of us on the boat that day knew the captain, and yet we followed his instructions without question. If you and I know the Lord, it should not be difficult to follow His plan for our lives as well. He is the One we can trust, no matter what situation we are facing.

Proverbs 3:1, "My son, do not forget my teaching, but keep my commands in your heart."

Do We Know Where to Look?

The water was calm as we pulled away from the dock, so I decided to make the run to a number twenty-two miles offshore. We arrived at our location and fished a few minutes, but the bite was slow. I told the fellows we would move to our next number, and reached for the ignition switch. Turning the key brought absolutely no sound. The engine did not turn over, there was no clicking to say the battery was weak...not a sound. All eyes turned and looked my way to see if I knew what was wrong. I told them to just keep fishing and I would check out what I felt might be the trouble.

The throttle control on the boat has a safety switch that keeps the engine from starting if it is in gear. Although the engine was not in gear, I felt sure there was something wrong with the safety switch. A few minutes later, they were relieved to hear the engine come to life, as the problem was corrected.

In our walk with the Lord, knowing where to look to get answers for our problems can be critical. A good knowledge of God's Word can help us find the answers we need. Not knowing what God has said or promised can leave us stranded in a difficult situation.

I knew where to look, so the problem with the engine was a quick and easy fix. The same can be true as we become more familiar with God's Word. God always makes a way of escape, but we need to be aware of where to look.

2 Timothy 2:15, "Study to show yourself approved unto God, a workman that needs not to be ashamed, rightly dividing the word of truth."

Appreciate the Small Things

The new couple visiting our church had stopped by the hospitality room after the service. The conversation had turned to fishing, and he began to tell me about something that had happened a few days before. He and his wife were fishing in a large lake, and because the wind was pushing the boat somewhat, they were getting too close to a pontoon boat. He reached to push them away, not realizing his wife was pushing at the same time. He lost his balance, and fell into the water. It was only about five feet deep, so when he came to the surface, he quickly pulled himself into the boat, only to realize his expensive prescription sun glasses were gone. The water was dark and murky, with grass on the bottom, so he knew they were lost.

They moved away to another fishing place, but later his wife encouraged him to go back and look for the glasses. Reluctantly, he did so, and when he got to the spot where he felt he had lost them, he threw a weighted plug with treble hooks to drag along the bottom. On the second try, the plug came in with one leg of the glasses caught on the hook. Was it coincidence or luck? He was giving God all the credit for helping him find those glasses. How quick are we to acknowledge the hand of God in a situation instead of calling it luck, or a coincidence? When we are quick to give thanks, and show appreciation for what God does in our lives, we place ourselves in a position to see God do even greater things!

1 Thessalonians 5:18, "In everything give thanks, for this is the will of God in Christ Jesus concerning you."

Having Choices is a Good Thing

One of the things that amazes me are the changes that have been made in fishing line over the past several years. "We have come a long way baby." Where once you only had a couple of choices in line, today there is a multiplicity of choices. Just to name a few, you have monofilament, braid, and fluorocarbon. Each of these comes in different colors, supposedly for differing conditions. You even have certain line that is better in high wind conditions, and in clear and murky water conditions. I'm not really sure how critical all this is, but many fishermen seem to believe in it.

How sad that we are so open to the different kinds of fishing lines to make us more effective in catching fish, and are so closed minded when it comes to the differing styles of churches and church services. If a fisherman can make a choice on what kind of fishing line to use, then why can't we, in the Church, understand that one size may not fit all when it comes to styles of service, types of music, or manner of preaching?

When the Word declares that, "I am God and I change not," it was not a reference to the stagnation of God in thought and ideas. That is seen in the many colors we find around us, and the differing landscapes in the world. God is a God of variety, and is not closed-minded to something new. The next time you go shopping for fishing line, or for the ladies...a different pair of shoes, or maybe a home church, thank God that you have more than one choice.

Isaiah 43:19a, “See, I am doing a new thing! Now it springs up; do you not perceive it?”

A New Anchor is Cheaper

It was my first time fishing at the mouth of the St. John's River. I was told that if I anchored close to the jetties, there were some huge red fish there. We dropped the anchor and began fishing. When we were ready to leave, we found the anchor was stuck in the rocks below. We pull and pulled, but it would not budge. I tied the anchor rope to the stern cleat, thinking I could pull it loose with the power of the boat. As the boat turned from the tension of the rope, it put our stern to the swells coming in from the Atlantic Ocean. Suddenly, a swell washed over the stern of the boat, and put over fifty gallons of water in the boat. I knew if that happened again, we would be in trouble. I quickly pulled my fillet knife and cut the anchor line, realizing the loss of the anchor was a minor thing.

Is your walk with Christ being placed in danger because of something you are anchored to? It may be a relationship, a habit, an attitude, or a practice in your life that allows the swells of the enemy to endanger your walk with the Lord. I had to make a choice that day, the anchor, or the boat and the lives of those with me. For me, the choice was a no-brainer...I could buy another anchor.

For you, the decision may not be as simple, but the choice is just as crucial. If you are not willing to cut loose from what is about to swamp your walk with Christ, you may go down, and take others with you.

Galatians 5:1b, "Stand firm, then, and do not let yourselves be burdened again by a yoke of slavery."

Is It Time For a Repower?

If you have ever ridden in a boat that is underpowered, you know how difficult it is to get it "on plane." Being on plane means the boat has reached its peak level of ride in the water, and is encountering the least amount of drag or resistance from the water. This makes the engine work easier, and the boat can then reach speeds not possible when the boat is off plane.

Sometimes, in our work for the Lord, it seems like we just can't get what we are doing up and going. The reason may be that you are attempting to do something for the Lord, but you are underpowered. We can spend so much time in the "doing" of what God has called us to, that we miss the opportunity to maintain and even increase our power in Christ. Although God is interested in what we are doing for the Kingdom, He is more interested in who we are becoming in the Kingdom. Time spent in personal prayer and devotion will always translate into more power, more effectiveness, and more success for the Kingdom of God.

Just as a boat that is underpowered will find it difficult to get on top and run effectively, a believer in Christ will also feel the pull and drag of this world when their spiritual life is underpowered. When a boat is underpowered and a change is made, we say it is being repowered. Does your life need to be repowered, so that you can become more effective for the Kingdom? Need something to get your work for God up and running more efficiently? Maybe the change needed is more power to get "on plane."

Acts 1:8a, "But you will receive power when the Holy Spirit comes on you."

Keep an Eye Out For Corrosion

Because my fishing is almost always in salt water, I am well aware of the harsh environment this presents for all the equipment I use. From the boat and motor to all the fishing tackle and the rods and reels, the salt water and the salt air can present a serious corrosion problem. No matter how long the day fishing has been, or how tired I am when I get back home, I cannot slack off and not thoroughly clean and properly lubricate everything. Taking the time at the end of the fishing day to properly care for the boat and equipment will mean it will be ready the next time I have an opportunity to go fishing. Putting it off until another time, or not doing it at all, is a sure way to allow corrosion to start that will cost me later.

Life lived in this world also places you and me, as believers, in a harsh and corrosive environment. Just as the boat and equipment needs to be cleaned and lubricated regularly, your life needs the constant infusion of God's Word, prayer, and the family of God, to keep the world's corrosion from our spiritual life. Putting off our personal devotion time with Christ, and our fellowship in the house of God, is just as serious for our spiritual life as putting off the cleaning of my boat and fishing equipment. Failure to properly care for your walk with Christ will definitely have a corrosive effect on your life, and you will not be prepared when the Holy Spirit calls on you to touch another life.

Psalms 86:11, "Teach me your way, LORD, that I may rely on your faithfulness; give me an undivided heart, that I may fear your name."

Is The Bilge Pump Working?

I pushed the throttle forward, but the sluggish reaction of the boat told me there was a problem. As I looked to see what was going on, I noticed the stern of the boat seemed to be setting lower in the water than normal. I opened the cover to the bilge area, and immediately knew that something was wrong. Somehow, we had taken on a considerable amount of water, and this, coupled with the fact that the automatic bilge pump had not come on, was causing the problem. I quickly turned on the manual pump switch, and was grateful to see a good stream of water shooting out through the bilge outlet.

Our lives are under constant attack from the enemy. Many times, we are not even aware of what affect he is having, until we try to get underway for something the Lord has called us to do. We may not realize that we have begun to harbor unforgiveness for what someone has done. We may not know that guilt has built a stronghold in our lives. What we have been watching, or become a part of on social media, may have allowed a large amount of the world's trash to build up in our bilge. Sometimes the "automatic" of our Christian walk just doesn't do the job. Just going through the motions of devotions, church attendance, or even prayer, is not working. We need to make a deliberate move to rid our lives of those things that are weighing us down spiritually. Set aside some time for serious prayer and fasting, and allow the Holy Spirit to empty your bilge area. You can get a fresh start!

Hebrews 12:1, "Let us throw off everything that hinders, and the sin that so easily entangles."

Watch for Fish Stealing Sharks

Susan's dad had joined me for some speckled trout fishing. We were on the flats near Anclote Island, and the fishing had been pretty good. I had just placed another nice speckled trout on the stringer, and hung the fish over the side. As I did, something caught my eye in the water a few feet away from the boat. When I looked closer, I saw a shark, at least ten feet long, and he was headed for the stringer of fish I had just put out. Needless to say, it did not take me but a second to pull the fish back into the boat, and deny the shark what he must have thought was an easy meal.

How often in our lives, because we have not remained vigilant, we have allowed the enemy to steal something of ours. It may have been just a sudden impulse to lie on that application, but the lie allowed the enemy to steal our integrity. Spending too much time with someone of the opposite sex can open a door that will allow the enemy to steal our family, and set us on a path of destruction.

We cannot prevent the enemy from cruising around the boat of our life, but we can guard the spiritual character traits that are ours through our relationship with Christ. The enemy does not need a large door to enter our heart; he only needs a crack in the spiritual armor we wear. Be aware of the cruising sharks!

2 Samuel 11:2-3, "One evening David got up from his bed, and walked around on the roof of the palace. From the roof, he saw a woman bathing. The woman was very beautiful, and David sent someone to find out about her."

Inexperience Is Not Forever

If you are having a boring day, or just need some humor in your life, drive down to the local boat ramp and watch as people attempt to launch or retrieve their boat from the water. It will be easy to determine those who have done this many times, and those who may possibly be a first timer, or at least new to boating. From the difficulty of just backing the trailer down to the water, to getting the boat to come off the trailer, the contortions and efforts of those new at this can bring some real excitement and humor to your day. I have seen cars dragged into the water, because the driver forgot to set the brake. There are situations when the boat begins to sink by the dock, because the plug was not put in. Of course all this is only humorous if you are the one watching, and not the one going through the experience.

Surely, God must have this same kind of feeling as He watches those who have recently given their life to Him go through some brand new experiences in the Christian faith. Those of us who have launched the boat hundreds of times seem to forget that we were also at one time new to the boating experience. Just as we "old salts" need to be a little more sympathetic to the new boater, maybe those of us who have served the Lord for many years need to try to remember back to when we were new in Christianity. We should cut some slack to the new Christians we are often so quick to criticize. A word of compassion, and a little understanding, can go a long way to encourage the new believer.

1Thessalonians 5:11, "Therefore encourage one another, and build each other up."

Judging a Fish by Its Name

When the fish was brought to the surface, I knew immediately that it was a lizard fish. I have caught many of these fish and have always considered them a trash fish species, something to be cut up for bait or discarded. However, after reading an article in a fishing magazine, I had learned that they were actually supposed to be very tasty. Because this one was almost 24 inches long, I decided to keep it, and give the lowly lizard fish a try. To my great delight and surprise, I found the article to be correct...they are delicious. All those fish that I had cut up for bait over the years could have actually been deep fried and eaten. Such a waste!

The same is true in our walk with Christ. Those individuals who seem to be obnoxious, those who just seem to love to create problems and situations in our lives, can prove to be a diamond in the rough. How many times have we judged someone without ever trying to understand what might be going on in his/her life? The lizard fish was always a trash fish to me, because I did not know the facts. I had listened to other people who said the same thing. That person in your workplace, the one who lives next door to you, or that relative you always avoid at reunions, may simply be in need of someone to care enough to look beyond preconceived notions, and love them as Jesus would. You really know you love the way Jesus did when you can love those you do not like.

John 13:35, "By this, everyone will know that you are my disciples, if you love one another."

Needing a Trim Adjustment

I watched the boat near us take off, and I knew right away that he had the engine trim way too high. The power tilt and trim on a boat engine are designed to help the motor achieve the most efficient position at different speeds. Having the trim too high on takeoff will cause the bow to rise sharply, making it difficult to see ahead of you, and difficult to get the boat on plane. After the boat is underway, raising the trim will help the boat climb higher in the water, and create less drag and resistance. A good boat operator will be constantly checking and adjusting the trim level to achieve optimum performance.

In our walk with God, we find that He is constantly making adjustments in our lives, also. Of course, we are much more comfortable when things remain familiar, and we encounter no real surprises. The Captain of our boat knows that allowing things to remain the same can bring stagnation in our relationship with Him, or can lull us into a comfort area that can quickly develop into a spiritual coffin for us.

The hand of our Savior is always on the trim switch of our lives, making the necessary changes that will allow us to reach optimum performance for Christ. Just as these choices are not left up to the boat to make as it thinks best, God does not leave these choices to you and me. When we are willing to surrender our lives to the control of the Holy Spirit, the Captain of our boat will make sure we are planed out and operating efficiently at all times.

Psalms 139:10, “Even there your hand will guide me, your right hand will hold me fast.”

No Braided Line on Board

The mate on the large party boat was watching me closely as I came aboard with my fishing rods. As I placed them where I would be fishing, he walked up and asked me a question: “You don’t have any braided line on those reels do you? We don’t allow any braided line on the boat.” I assured him there was no braided line on the reels, and then asked him why they had that rule, when braided line is legal to use and popular. He explained to me the braided line is very strong, and because it has an ultra-small diameter for its strength, people can often be cut by the line if they grab it without gloves. He said one of the mates on the boat almost lost a finger when he grabbed a braided line to pull in a large amberjack, and the fish made a hard lunge to free itself.

There are also areas in our Christian lives that may not be wrong, but could present a real danger to others who may not have the same spiritual maturity. As followers of Jesus, we should never allow our freedom in Christ to become a stumbling block for others. Our position on alcohol, movies, the way we dress, and a multitude of other things that may not seem to be a problem for our lives, could be a stumbling block for someone who is struggling in their walk with the Lord. The real love of Christ will be willing to make sacrifices, and help others in their spiritual growth, even when it is not convenient for us.

Romans 14: 21, “It is better not to eat meat or drink wine, or to do anything else that will cause your brother or sister to fall.”

It Takes More Than Gel-Coat

While driving past the boat dealership, I was amazed at the many different colors on the boats. When I first started owning boats, many years ago, there were only a couple of colors available. Now there are many colors to choose from, almost any color you can imagine. Oddly enough, the color coat or gel-coat is the first part of the boat hull to be put in the mold. It is only after this gel coat layer is installed that the fiberglass matting and resin is carefully layered into the boat hull. It is in these layers of matting and resin that the hull of the boat gets its strength. The pretty color gel-coat adds little, if any, real strength to the boat. The structural strength is simply covered by the gel coat to make the boat attractive, and allow the resin to dry hard. A boat needs much more than a pretty coating to have real structural integrity.

The same reality exists in our Christian life. We can put on our pretty faces, all smiles and sweetness, but that will mean very little unless there is true love and integrity underneath. It also takes more than the outwardly observed forms of spirituality to give strength and quality to our walk with God. Sometimes what others see on the outside does not really reflect what is on the inside. Like the gel-coat of the boat, if the exterior of our lives is not provided with a sound structural foundation, it will sooner or later crack and create a major problem. The real strength and integrity of our walk with Christ is found in those quiet, and often unseen times, we spend alone with Him.

1Samuel 16:7b, "People look at the outward appearance, but the Lord looks at the heart."

Only if the Weather is Good

As an offshore fisherman, one of the important things to keep a constant eye on is the weather. When I am planning a trip for the weekend, I check the marine forecast at the first of the week. I continue to monitor the forecast to see if something might show up that wasn't apparent at the first of the week. Many times, what appears to be a great forecast initially turns bad, as I continue checking it out a few days later. All the plans made, based on what I saw at first, must be changed, because the weather has changed.

I have found the same thing true in my choices in life. Sometimes, what I am looking at will seem fine in the beginning, but as I come closer to making the decision, or move in a certain direction, the view begins to get clearer and things are not as I first believed. You and I can make plans, based on what we know, but, as time continues, we recognize that we did not have enough, or even accurate information.

Thank God, He will help us make right choices and good decisions. We must keep our eyes on Him, and see what He is trying to show us. I have actually gotten up on the morning of the fishing trip and called the fellows to cancel, because what I thought the weather was going to be proved wrong. Do not be afraid to change your mind. Keep an eye on what God is trying to show you, and He will help you make the best decisions for your life.

Deuteronomy 32:4, "He is the Rock, His works are perfect, and all His ways are just. A faithful God who does no wrong, upright and just is He."

I Don't Want a Remote Reel

We live in a world where we are obsessed with a remote control for everything. We have a TV remote, a remote for the ceiling fan, even remote-controlled fire places. They now have a remote control for the trolling motor. The remote has given birth to people who want to put out as little effort as possible in their life.

As an avid fisherman, I'm waiting for someone to invent a remote control for the fishing rod and reel. Just push the button and set the hook. Push another button and engage the reel and bring the fish in. Are you kidding me? I want to feel the power and weight of the fish when I set the hook. I want to pit my skill and strength against the fish, as I turn the handle of the reel and pull against the fish.

The sad thing is that many of us find our relationship with God is more of the remote-controlled type than real hands on. We want the preacher to pray for us, study the Word, teach us what it says to do, and even lay hands on us so we can receive something from the Lord. Many have even resorted to seeking someone to give them a word from God. Seems a little like remote-control religion. The problem with remote-controlled religion is that we miss the special closeness and intimacy that makes our life in Christ so special. Just as a remote-controlled relationship with our spouse would not work, neither will it work in our relationship with Christ. Put down the remote religion, and get up close and intimate with Jesus Christ. It will change your life!

James 4:8, "Come near to God, and He will come near to you."

What You Don't See Can Hurt

People in the fishing industry are always looking for something new that will give the fisherman an advantage over the fish. One product that is fairly new on the market, and designed to do just that, is fluorocarbon line. It is stronger, abrasive-resistant, and practically invisible in the water. It is used primarily as leader material running from the regular line to the hook, hopefully making it more difficult for the fish to recognize the danger lurking ahead.

Just as fishermen are constantly on the lookout for something that will give them an advantage over the fish, the enemy of our soul is always on the lookout for a better way to manipulate and deceive the child of God. When you and I fail to maintain the proper vigilance in our spiritual life, Satan may present some bait that does not seem to be dangerous, but it is attached to something that will ruin our lives. That new co-worker of the opposite sex may seem harmless, but does that relationship have a fluorocarbon leader attached to a path that will lead to destruction? That financial decision may seem harmless enough, but have you missed the fluorocarbon leader that may attach it to a controlling debt? The small lie may seem inconsequential, but it can come back to bite you when you least expect it.

The enemy is a master at presenting a temptation in a way in which the danger involved is almost invisible. Trust the voice of the Lord, and look beyond the obvious to what might bring destruction to your life.

1Peter 5:8, "Be alert and of sober mind. Your enemy the devil prowls around like a roaring lion looking for someone to devour."

Wisdom in Setting the Drag

I knew the fish was large, and the drag on the reel was just not tight enough to slow it down. The difficult choice now would be, "Do I tighten the drag so I can prevent the fish from taking all the line off the reel, or do I just hold on hoping the fish tires before the line runs out?" Of course, if I tighten the drag, I take a chance the power of the fish will break the line. Every fisherman has faced this quandary, some making the right choice and landing the fish, and for others, the fish gets away.

All of us who have children have faced this same kind of situation in raising our sons or daughters. They have reached the age where they want a little more freedom, or maybe a lot more freedom. They are straining at the control of your choices and decisions, wanting to make their own choices. The question faced by every parent is, "How tight should the drag be?" If we tighten it too much, they may break away totally. If we loosen it too much, that could mean serious consequences, also. The problem is that there is no answer that fits all situations, and, certainly, all children are not alike.

The fisherman has to go on gut instinct, and, hopefully, the experience he has. For a parent, gut instinct helps, but we can also call on the Lord for His wisdom and direction. When the kids start straining at the drag, seek the Lord first; because your decision on how much drag to use is critical.

James 1:5, "If any of you lacks wisdom, you should ask God, who gives generously to all without finding fault, and it will be given to you."

The Reel Can Make a Difference

I was using an open-face spinning reel and rod, and was able to cast quite a ways from the back of the head boat. I had caught several fish in the same location a number of yards behind the boat. The young teen standing next to me wanted to fish in the same area, but he was using a very large level wind reel not designed for casting. Undaunted by that fact, he proceeded to try, and cast to the location where I was catching the fish. The lead and bait came to a sudden halt, and I looked over to see a huge "bird nest" of fishing line on the reel. It would take several minutes, and maybe even a pocketknife to untangle the line so the young man could fish again.

What seemed like a good idea had gone very badly, because the young man did not understand the limitations of his reel. Each of us has probably faced a similar situation in life. Decisions made from what might have been the best of intentions, suddenly go south on us. Our lives are now backlashed and in a tangled mess. Sometimes we are not experienced enough in certain areas to make the choice or decision that we need to make. Whatever the scenario that got us where we are in our lives, we need the Lord to help us untangle the "Bird Nest." The wonderful message is that He will help us. It may require some time, and even some work with a "pocketknife" from the Holy Spirit. Don't panic! God is here to help. He will soon have you back fishing again.

1Peter 5:7, "Cast all your anxiety on Him, because He cares for you. "

Things Change for a Reason

Fishing had slowed down, so I told the fellows to pull in their lines and we would move to another spot. When I turned the key to start the motor, there was not even a sound. I began to check things out, and, several minutes later, the engine fired up. I told the men that it might be better to go back in until I could figure out what was wrong. I have to say I was not a happy camper, and the fellows were also disappointed. When I got the boat home, I was just starting the cleaning process when my cell phone rang. It was my youngest brother, Steve, who lives in Georgia. His words hit hard, as he told me that my other brother, David, who lives near Steve, had been rushed to the hospital. The doctor was saying that things were very serious, and the family might need to be called in.

It was only later that I realized that I would not have been able to receive that call if I was still fifteen miles offshore. What I saw as an aggravating circumstance was really the divine hand of God taking care of things in my life.

Whatever you are facing in your life today, let me assure you that God is in control, and He is working His plan for your life. Even if you are in a situation caused by your bad choices, God will accomplish His best for you. You need to turn it all over to Him, and do His will.

What appeared to be a ruined fishing trip was really a divine intervention from God.

Romans 8:28, "And we know that in all things God works for the good of those who love Him, who have been called according to His purpose."

Who's Following in Your Wake?

The fog was heavy, and my son, Kenny, did not have a GPS on his boat. He needed to follow me out and back for our fishing trip. All went well at first, but I suddenly realized that I did not see his boat behind me. I slowed down and eventually stopped, hoping to hear the sound of his engine, or see his boat coming out of the heavy fog. It seemed longer than it was, but he finally emerged out of the fog and pulled up beside us. I asked him how he had found us in the fog, and he replied, "I followed your wake." The wake is the trail the boat leaves in the water as it progresses forward. The life you and I live also leaves a wake. The choices and decisions we make, the words and actions that define our life, leave a wake that is easily seen by our children and others who may be close to us. Life is not something we can live for our own purposes, and forget about those for whom we are responsible. Our children are directly affected by our choices, especially as they follow in the "wake" we leave in life.

Kenny later bought a GPS, and did not need to follow me. Our children will also become adults, and make their own choices and decisions in life. No matter how old they are, the effect of the wake of your life will always be with them. They may get out of the house and live on their own, but your wake can still be a guiding factor in their lives.

Proverbs 22:6, "Train up a child in the way he should go, and when he is old, he will not depart from it."

A Consequence for the Bait

I had placed the rod in the rod holder, and turned to cut up some more bait. My dad told me something was on the line but I knew it was just a grunt, so I told him I would get it in a minute. Suddenly, the drag on the reel began to scream, because something very large had grabbed the struggling grunt. I gave the rod to my brother, so he could fight the fish. About forty five minutes later, a six foot Black Tip shark was alongside the boat. The grunt had fallen prey to a small piece of cut bait, but, when hooked, he had become the bait for the large shark.

How many times have we seen the same thing in life? We, or someone we know, fall for the bait of the enemy, then make a choice or decision that gets a grip on our lives. Because of our choice, we become vulnerable to many other deceptions, some much larger than we can defend ourselves against. I'm sure the grunt never expected to become the bait for a shark. I'm sure the shark, as well, never anticipated the sharp hook penetrating its jaw.

When we fall for the deception of the enemy, we are never thinking about what the final consequences might be. Maybe you are being drawn in a particular direction right now, and you need to take a moment and really examine where all this might be leading you.

That day turned out to be a bad day for the grunt, and, also for the shark. Tomorrow could turn out to be a bad day for you, if you don't make the right decisions today.

Haggai 1:5, "Now this is what the Lord Almighty says, "Give careful thought to your ways."

Hooks Are a Part of Any Lure

As I walked up and down the aisles of the fishing department ,I was amazed at the variety of different fishing lures and baits on the shelves. There were jigs, top water plugs, soft baits, spinner baits, and the list goes on. Not only were there different kinds of lures, there was just about every color in the color spectrum. Could fish really be so dim-witted as to see all of these as possible food? Of course, not all of these are as successful as others, but you, at least, have your choice.

The world around us is much like the bait in the fishing tackle department. There are so many different allurements to entice us, and lead us away from our walk with the Lord. Sin offers access to almost anything our human nature might desire. If we are looking for it, Satan will make sure it is available.

Just as with any fishing lure or bait, those things offered by the world also come with a nasty surprise. There are always one or more hooks attached. The enemy is never satisfied with just luring us to his bait; he wants to set a hook into our lives that can ultimately destroy us. Just as a fishing lure is presented in a way as to attract a fish, the enticements of the world are presented by the enemy to attract you and me. Just as a fishing lure's ultimate goal is to catch the unwary fish, the goal of Satan is to catch the unwary believer. The only safety for the fish is to stay away from the lure. The same is true in your life and mine.

James 1:14, "But every man is tempted, when he is drawn away of his own lust, and enticed."

The Back Wash Is Real

Cary backed the trailer down the ramp for me to drive the boat up on it. I was approaching slowly, lining the boat up with the guides on the trailer. Suddenly, I felt the boat move hard sideways, completely throwing me off alignment with the trailer. I looked to see what had happened, I realized that the large ferry that takes people to the casino boat offshore had put their engines in gear, and the prop wash created the turbulence that moved me sideways.

The same can often be true in our lives. We seem to have everything lined up, and we are moving forward with confidence, then, all of a sudden, we are thrown completely off track. All the plans, even the directions that we believed came from God, are suddenly out of sorts. The job that had sustained your family for years downsizes, the regular checkup at the doctor is bad news, or one of your children calls to say your grandchild is very ill. The list of things that can suddenly broadside us could go on and on.

The question is not what was suddenly forced upon your life, but what will be your response to it? David hears his son is riding to Jerusalem to take the throne of Israel by force. Paul and Silas are placed in a Philippian jail. We are not promised that life will always go as planned, but what we are promised is that God will be there for us.

I had to make some adjustments that day. I had to reposition the boat, but we got it on the trailer. You may have to make some adjustments, but trust in the One who promised to never leave you and you will get back on track.

Joshua 1:5b, “I will never leave you, nor forsake you.”

Follow the Markers For Safety

Having been a boater most of my life, I am acquainted with the rules of the waterways, and especially what the channel markers are for. Even if you are not used to a particular area, if you know the meaning of the markers and the colors they are painted, you should have no trouble navigating the channel. A little thing I use to remind me is “green right going, red right returning.” Having good channel markers to map out the course for you on the water can be useful, and prevent damage to your boat by running aground or on an oyster bar.

The heavenly Father was also good enough to give us channel markers in the Word of God to facilitate navigating through life. The principles and directions found in God’s Word are there to help us make the choices that will keep us from running aground, or, worse yet, colliding with an oyster bar and ripping a hole in our lives. Just as some boaters feel they can do fine without the red and green channel markers, there are many people that seem to think they can navigate through life without reading and following the channel markers in God’s word.

We can stumble through life making choices based on what we think is right, but we will find that there are oyster bars and pitfalls everywhere. The path you choose may seem quicker, or even easier, but it also may have an oyster bar right in the middle of it. Stay with the channel markers found in the Word of God; you will find your life following God’s path where the blessings are awaiting you.

Psalms 119:105, “Your Word is a lamp for my feet, a light on my path.”

Red Lights for a Reason

I was coming into the dock, when I noticed the boat that was tied up there was positioned in such a way that no one else could use the dock area. To make matters worse, there was no one in the boat to move it up or back a little. With the wind blowing briskly and the current moving with the incoming tide, it would not be safe to approach the dock with no clear place to tie up the boat. I would just have to wait until the boat owner came back and moved. I am probably the only person who wonders how some people can be so blind to what is going on around them. For example, you are trying to drive down the parking lot lane, and the person walking just has to walk right in the center of the isle. Why can't the person getting ready to pay their bill at the grocery store ever consider that it would save everyone time if they had their money or credit card out and ready to use.

They say patience is a virtue. I'm sure they are right, but it is a virtue that most of us struggle to acquire. Let me encourage you, though, that just because something is difficult, it does not excuse you and me from seeking God's help in achieving it. A recent study showed that when we stop to appreciate people and things around us, we find our satisfaction with life is greater. Maybe sometimes God just wants us to slow down, and smell the roses along the way. Be thankful for what God allows in life.

Romans 8:28, "And we know that in all things God works for the good of those who love Him, who have been called according to His purpose."

Handle the Fish with Care

If you have watched the fishing programs that are becoming quite popular on TV and YouTube, I'm sure you have seen the pros, and others, releasing many of the fish they catch. I'm amazed at how gently they handle the fish, and how they make sure the fish is totally revived before they release it to swim away. When a fish is caught in deep water, they realize they must vent the fish before releasing it, so it can swim back to its deep-water home. Of course, their goal is to sustain the fishery, so that the sport can continue.

It reminds me somewhat of God's dealings with us when He has allowed us to face a time of trial or difficulty. There is so much tenderness and mercy in what God will do in our lives to make sure we have come through the difficulties without any spiritual injuries. His compassion for us can be seen in the way He puts people around us to encourage us and stand with us, as we are getting back on our feet. He will also allow the Holy Spirit to help us release all the anger, frustration, and hurt that the situation may have caused to build up in our heart. The trial was never intended to destroy us.

We may not always understand the reason or purpose behind the trial we have faced, but God is faithful to help us walk through it with victory. Be faithful to God, and He will release you very carefully to "swim" again in His love and favor.

Romans 5:5, "And hope does not put us to shame, because God's love has been poured out into our hearts through the Holy Spirit, who has been given to us."

The Wake Will Tell You

The sun was not up yet, and the moon and stars were nowhere to be seen. Even with the compass and GPS, in these conditions it can be really difficult to determine if you are moving on a straight course. When headed west in the Gulf of Mexico, there are no markers to fix on. I have found a way to know if the boat is traveling straight, or is moving off course. I simply look behind me at the wake of the boat. Even in the dim light, the water emits a glow and you can see the previous path of the boat very well. Life can put you in the same dilemma at times. There may not be sufficient light, or even spiritual markers ahead of you to make sure you are following a straight path. Even people around you offering advice may not be enough to assure you that you are headed straight on the path God has laid out for you. Just take a look behind you, and see what the wake you are leaving is telling you. The wake will never lie. It will show exactly where you have been, and if you are running a straight course.

The enemy loves to bring spiritual darkness around us that prevents us from seeing clearly our course in life. God is faithful to help us, if we are willing to keep an eye on the wake we have created. Looking back can help us to keep a clear perspective...we can see what our life is accomplishing. Looking back on our wake will help us keep our course straight.

Proverbs 4:18, "The path of the righteous is like the morning sun, shining ever brighter till the full light of day."

You Need the Anchor in Front

There are many safety factors that you should be aware of when boating. One thing that can easily be taken for granted is the proper way to anchor a boat. When the water is calm, and there is little wind or waves, you can tie the anchor off in the front or the rear of the boat; it will make little or no difference. That is not true if the winds are high, and the current or the waves are strong. In that case, it is very important that you tie the anchor off at the front of the boat. The front of the boat is designed to ride up and over the incoming waves, and does not have the heavy weight of the engine to contend with. Properly anchored and tied off, your boat is designed to handle substantially more rough water from the front than if tied off in the stern.

We find the same is true in our spiritual lives. Having our life properly anchored and "tied off" to the Son of God can determine how safely we will ride out the winds and waves that confront us. Tying our spiritual anchor off in the front of your life means that Jesus is out front, and He is leading the way. When we tie the anchor off in the stern, it means that we are making the choices and decisions, and trusting in our own wisdom as we face the storms of life.

When we are properly anchored in Christ, no matter which way the storms of life come at us, we will be facing them "bow on" with Jesus in control of every decision we make.

Hebrews 6:19, "We have this hope as an anchor for the soul, firm and secure."

Low Tide Can Strand You

Susan and I had made the short run in the boat to the sand bar north of Anclote Island. As I approached the East side of the sand bar to anchor the boat in position, I took note of where the tide level was. As I moved the boat in position, I noticed another boat that was completely stranded on shore, out of the water. Apparently, the owner had tied the boat up at high tide, and failed to keep a close watch on it as the tide was receding. His lack of attention to the tide now meant he would have a few hours to wait before he could hopefully refloat the boat again.

The same can be true when we fail to keep a close watch on our spiritual walk. We can get involved in life itself, and fail to recognize that our walk and relationship with God is being neglected. Maybe we are not praying as we should, or we are not in the Word of God regularly. Our attendance at church, perhaps, becomes sporadic. Suddenly, we are faced with a trying situation, and we find our spiritual boat is high and dry on the sand bar.

Thankfully, it does not need to be a permanent situation. We can simply go back to the basics of our faith, and begin rebuilding our relationship with Christ. Quite often, the difficulty we experienced was simply God's way of prodding us to check and see what the tide was doing in our life. Maintaining your walk with God is not an automatic thing; it takes being aware of what is going on in your life.

Mark 14:38, "Watch and pray so that you will not fall into temptation. The spirit is willing, but the flesh is weak."

Recognizing the Pinfish Trap

I had the fishing trip offshore planned for the next day, and was placing my pinfish traps out so we could have some live bait for the trip. Pinfish traps are wire baskets with a place in the center for the bait, and two or more places where the small pinfish can enter to get to the bait. The entry hole is wide initially, but narrows to channel the pinfish inside and then make it difficult for them to find an escape. Because the pinfish are attracted by the bait, they do not recognize the danger faced once inside the trap.

We have all faced pinfish traps in our own lives. You know what I mean, those things that are so easy to get involved in, but, as we go further, the path narrows and channels us into a trap. That sight on the internet that catches our attention, or that decision to talk a little longer with a person of the opposite sex. The bait can keep us so blinded to the danger that we fail to turn around before it's too late. We can thank God, His mercy and forgiveness is always there when we cry out, but it may not eliminate the pain and suffering we have to go through, or that we put others through because of our choices.

Sometimes our choices will shut doors in our lives that can never be opened again. When you find you are being attracted by something that you know is contrary to God's word, stop a minute and look around you. Could this be a pinfish trap set up to destroy you?

Proverbs 4:14, "Do not set foot on the path of the wicked, or walk in the way of evildoers."

What Lurks Beneath the Buoy?

It was still dark when I pointed the boat west, and headed out to our first fishing spot fourteen miles away. I turned on the million-candle power Black Max spotlight in order to watch for the crab trap buoys that dot the water in our area. The Styrofoam ball floating on the surface poses little danger to the boat or motor, but it's attached to a rope that is attached to a wire crab trap. If the motor hits one, sometimes the propeller will cut the rope. The only problem is the crabber may find it difficult to locate his trap. If the propeller doesn't cut the rope, the rope will often wrap around the propeller, and pull the crab trap up rapidly, posing a danger to the boat and motor. Being diligent to watch for and avoid the Styrofoam balls allows you to avoid the danger lurking below.

God has also given us the light of His word to help us locate the dangers Satan has set out along our path. We may not always recognize the danger the Word is talking about, but, if we fail to heed the warning, we will quickly find that what is on the surface is attached to something that is unseen and dangerous to our lives. God's Word will illuminate the buoy, but you and I must then be ready to move away from the danger.

Do not get distracted and miss the buoy! You will then realize...too late...that you are now caught in the crab trap. Watch for the crab buoys, and give them a wide birth.

Psalms 140:5, "The arrogant have hidden a snare for me; they have spread out the cords of their net and have set traps for me along my path."

The Value in the Fishing Rods

I saw the garage sale sign, and could not resist the urge to see what they might have. After looking around, I spotted a number of fishing rods in the corner. I knew at once that they were old, and had not been used in a long time. A couple of the rods were missing the guides, and the others displayed the corrosion that always comes with neglect or lack of use. The elderly man also must have recognized their lack of value, as he told me I could have them all for $5.00.

How often do we allow our relationship with the Lord to deteriorate to the same extent? We have not really spent any time in His Word, our prayer life is little or non-existent, and our time being used in the Kingdom of God just never seems to happen. Spiritually, our lives are just stacked in the corner, obviously of little value to us or anyone else.

The problem then comes when someone asks us about our Christian life. Just as the value the man saw in his fishing equipment was obvious, the value we place on our relationship with Christ will also be obvious. Don't allow the enemy to rob you of the most important relationship in your life. Place a high value on your prayer time, your time in the Word, and your time in spiritual service for the Kingdom of God. If you do, people will easily be able to see the value you place on your life in Christ. You never know when someone may be shopping for that relationship in his/her own life.

Mark 12:30, "Love the Lord your God with all your heart and with all your soul and with all your mind and with all your strength."

Be Sure Before You Use the Saw

Fiberglass chips began to fly as I pressed the blade of the power saw into the front deck of the Wellcraft Step V-20. I had pondered the project for some time, but now there was no going back... the saw was making sure of that. With each inch of cut the saw made, the opportunity of changing my mind about the decision to open the front bow of the boat was taken away.

The same is true in life, as well. Whether we have put the proper time and thought into our decisions or not, some of the decisions we make will have consequences that will affect our lives permanently. Quitting school before we are finished, having sex before marriage, marrying outside of our faith, aborting the child we did not feel ready for, are all decisions that will have a lasting effect. Often the pain and problems caused by these choices must be dealt with by not only us, but many who are involved in our lives. We can find forgiveness from God, and people, but that does not always change the consequences of the choices we have made. They will remain a constant reminder of those choices.

My choice to remove the front deck of the boat worked out great. Sad to say, not all my choices have worked out quite so well. We need to remember, before we make a decision, that the decision will have consequences, some which we will never be able to change. Make sure that the decisions in your life follow the will of God, and He will be responsible for the consequences.

Isaiah 7:15, "He will be eating curds and honey when he knows enough to reject the wrong and choose the right."

The Protection of the Oil

I knew the throttle cable running back to the carburetor of the boat's inboard/outboard engine would not fare well if exposed to the salt air for too long. It was not made of stainless steel, so being exposed to the salt air would make it susceptible to corrosion. I came up with a plan I felt would prevent the exposure and corrosion. I found a small plastic tube the cable would fit through, and put oil in the tube. I then inserted the throttle cable into the tube with the oil, and sealed the ends of the tube around the ends of the cable with small clamps, encasing the cable in a blanket of oil. The wire of the cable could then move freely, but the outer shield of the cable was protected by the layer of oil all around it.

Our lives are always facing the corroding effect of the world around us. Left exposed and unprotected, we will quickly find the influences of the world creating problems and the corrosion that will ruin our testimony for Christ. The answer is to allow the oil of the Holy Spirit to surround your life with His anointing and protection. He can provide the needed barrier between you and the world that will allow you to have a positive effect on those around you without allowing their lives to bring corrosion to your walk with Christ.

The cable on the boat remained loose and working for a long time, because of the oil that surrounded it. With the power of the Holy Spirit surrounding you, your life can be all God has ordained it to be.

1John 2:20, "But you have an anointing from the Holy One, and all of you know the truth."

Is Dead Bait Floating on Top?

For those wanting to use live bait when fishing, there are two features of a live well that are crucial. The first is the need to maintain a good flow of water in and out of the live well. This is critical to provide a good oxygen supply for the bait in the live well. The second is to make sure the corners of the live well are round, allowing no place for the bait to crowd in too tightly, robbing them of needed oxygen.

The Church acts much like a live well for the Kingdom of God. Christ wants our lives to be the bait that attracts the world to God's Kingdom. If the Church is to be effective, there must be a good flow of the Holy Spirit for us to live in. When the Church allows for the moving of the Holy Spirit, He will energize our lives to draw the world to Christ. When that flow is stymied, weakness, and even death, can follow. The church was never intended to be just a place where believers could congregate. Church members who sit on pews and do nothing are like live bait congregating in the corner of a live well, seeking safety and security, but only finding suffocation and death.

To keep bait alive and useful, you need to keep the water flowing and the bait in constant motion. To keep the Church healthy, you need to keep the Spirit of God flowing and the people busy doing the work of the Kingdom. You know the live well is not working properly when you see dead or dying bait coming to the surface. Enough said!

Mark 16:15, "He said to them, 'Go into all the world, and preach the gospel to all creation.'"

Are Rocks Below The Surface?

It would be our first time launching the boat at the park located near the mouth of the Weeki Wachee River. As we eased out into the channel, we could see what appeared to be PVC pipe sticking up in various places across the grass flats. As we approached one, we quickly found they were placed there as a warning of the rocks located just below the surface of the water. Later that day, we would realize that we also needed to watch closely for rocks that were not marked, or the marker was no longer there. As long as we were careful and kept a close watch on where we were going, there should be no problem.

God has been faithful to mark out many of the areas of danger in life that we may encounter. However, there are other dangers not as clearly defined. The culture we live in, also, has removed the markers. Just because the culture does not recognize the dangers that are lurking all around us, does not mean they are not there. You and I need the wisdom and guidance of the Holy Spirit to help us navigate through the submerged, hidden dangers that are around us. If we stay sensitive to His voice, and attentive to the directions found in the Word of God, we can enjoy the life God has given us, and achieve the goals He has set for us.

Dangers may be present, but we can navigate around them. Failure to heed the warnings of the markers will mean real heartache, and possibly disaster, in our lives. Pretending there is no danger is foolhardy, and may sink our testimony for the Lord.

Proverbs 4:11, "I instruct you in the way of wisdom, and lead you along straight paths."

Trim Tabs Help Keep it Level

I was looking forward to the trip offshore, not only for the day of fishing, but to try out the new trim tabs I had installed on the boat. Trim tabs are small flat pieces of metal, in my case 9" by 18", attached to the stern of the boat that help keep the boat level and stabilized. They are usually moved by a hydraulic cylinder. If the boat is listing to one side because of more weight on that side, a gentle touch of the switch and the downward movement of the trim tab will lift the boat back to level. The tabs can also help if you are going into heavy seas by keeping the bow down and cutting into the wave instead of bouncing across the top.

God has placed a set of spiritual "trim tabs" in Christian life. One side is the Word of God, and the other side are the spiritual leaders He has placed over us. Between these two, the balance in our spiritual lives can be maintained. No matter how far our lives may be listing one way or the other, a gentle touch from either of these can bring us back to a level place. They can also be the means of helping us cut through the trials and difficulties of life, instead of just bouncing around with little control.

Just as the trim tabs on the boat are controlled by the captain of the boat, God is the one at the controls of the trim tabs in our lives. Let Him do the adjusting, and life will be smoother and more level for you.

Isaiah 26:7, "The path of the righteous is level; you, the Upright One, make the way of the righteous smooth."

Learn to Enjoy the Gift

I opened the box that my youngest son had given to me, and was surprised to see the underwater LED fish attracting light. Fishermen have known for years that a light placed in the water under your boat or dock at night can be a great asset in attracting fish to your location. The light came with a long cord and battery clips to attach it to the power source in the boat. I was excited about the opportunity that the light offered to do some night fishing.

Jesus has given us a gift, that, when used properly, can be a powerful attractant to the world around us. When Christ comes into our lives, He comes with a powerful light of love and the Gospel message that He wants us to utilize to attract the lost and hurting to Him. However, unless we are willing to remove that light from the box, connect it to the power source of the Holy Spirit, and put it into the darkness of the world around us, it will have no effect.

Just as my son would be disappointed if I never utilized the gift he gave me, how must Jesus feel when you and I fail to utilize the light He has provided in our life?

Let me challenge you to remove the light in your life from its box, attach it to the power of the Holy Spirit, lower it into the darkness around you, and watch what happens. I believe you will be amazed at how your life, empowered by the Holy Spirit can attract people to Christ.

Acts 13:47, "For this is what the Lord has commanded us: 'I have made you a light for the Gentiles, that you may bring salvation to the ends of the earth.'"

Maintenance is a Cheap Fix

Having owned a boat most of my married life, I have heard many times, "A boat is a hole in the water you throw money into." I don't believe that has to be true. I have learned that lack of attention to small details in caring for a boat sets you up for larger problems. We use our cars often, so we tend to keep a pretty sharp eye on their maintenance and care. Because the boat is used less, maintenance is not something we always take seriously.

Maintenance also plays a vital part in our spiritual lives. That area we examine and care for regularly seems to operate without much difficulty. When we spend the needed time and energy on our marriages, we often find the problems that could become larger are taken care of quickly, saving a great deal of hurt and pain.

I can't tell you how many people with boats seldom take the time to clean and flush the engine, or place a cover over the boat to keep the trash and leaves out. These are simple maintenance items that we must attend to regularly if we are to prevent future problems.

In our marriages, we need to regularly clean and flush those habits and attitudes that can corrupt our love for our spouses. We need to keep a protective cover over our relationships, so the world cannot dump its trash in, and destroy our love for one another. This is just as true in our spiritual lives. Proper maintenance in your marriage and your spiritual life will allow you to be one of those who receive many blessings from the Lord.

Hebrews 2:3, "How shall we escape if we neglect so great a salvation?"

A Loose Clamp Can Sink You

I had been fishing for a couple of hours on the grass flats, and it was time to head back in. I hit the starter on the small 20-horse-power outboard, and turned the throttle on the tiller arm. The boat jumped forward, and I knew it would not take long to get back in. Suddenly, I felt a strange movement in the engine, and looked back to see it twisting on the transom as one of the screw locks holding it in place had worked loose. It was all I could do to shut the engine down, and prevent it from falling into the water as it slipped off the transom. I got it reattached, but, because it had gotten wet, it took a long time before I could get it started again. The short trip in became a two hour ordeal.

How often have we found our lives turned upside down by something that seemed small at first, but turned out to be a lot more than we expected. The fasting screw on the engine was not something I was in the habit of checking regularly. That is also true of our walk with Christ. When we fail to care for the seemingly small things in our walk with the Lord, the enemy can suddenly turn them into major problems. That broken relationship can become bitterness and unforgiveness. That small lie can later require more serious lies to be necessary. That casual stop at an internet site can lead to an addiction that can control your life.

Don't overlook the small things that give the enemy an opportunity to create a big thing.

Song of Solomon 2:15, "Catch for us the foxes, the little foxes that ruin the vineyards, our vineyards that are in bloom."

Chalk it up to Inexperience

Our new youth pastor, Jamie, had joined me for a day on the grass flats, looking to catch some trout. I knew he was somewhat new to this kind of fishing, so I spent the first few minutes showing him a few things I felt he would need to know. We finally tied on the lead head hooks, picked out the color jig we wanted to use, and began casting the baits. It looked like it would be a great day, and a fun time out on the water together. All of a sudden, I felt a hard and shape pain in the back of my head. I reached for the area of my head where the pain was coming from, and realized there was a lead head jig stuck in my scalp. My youth pastor was apologizing profusely as I extracted the hook from where it had stuck in me.

If you have been a part of the Kingdom of God very long, you have found that Christian people can often bring pain and difficulty to your life. Many times, when they are young in Christ and inexperienced in their walk with the Lord, they can make choices and decisions that hurt others. We need to be careful that we do not over-react to these situations, as we could damage their commitment to Christ.

We can all look back on a time, when we were young in Christ, and didn't always understand that the jig head we were throwing might hurt someone if we weren't careful. Be patient and forgiving, and you will teach that new Christian a valuable lesson in life. That young man is now pastoring a great church.

James 1:19, "Everyone should be quick to listen, slow to speak, and slow to become angry."

Trying to Fix Our Own Motor?

I have always done much of the maintenance on my outboards, so when the boat's engine began intermittently not starting, I was sure I could fix it. Besides, I knew it would not be cheap at the dealer. With my tester, I traced the wires and checked every connection from the switch back to the engine. I found that, for some reason, the wire intended to energize the starter solenoid was going into the power pack on the engine with twelve volts, but coming out with no voltage. I decided I would jump the wire before it went into the power pack, taking it directly to the solenoid. It worked, and the engine was starting every time. It worked fine for a few days out fishing, but, one day, the check engine gauge on the Etec outboard came on. Not having a way to test that, I had to take it in for service. The first thing the tech wanted to know was why I had changed the wiring connections.

We try to fix the problems in our lives, without taking the problem to the only One who knows how to fix us. We tinker around, and, before long, the engine warning light of our heart comes on. We know that we need to get to our spiritual heavenly Father for some real analysis.

The outboard technician was able to figure out the problem quickly and repair the engine. Even though there was a charge, I was grateful to be able to use the boat again with confidence.

Don't tinker around trying to fix something that only God can correct. Pay the price, and let God get you back into life with confidence.

Psalms 119:73, "Your hands made me and formed me."

Lines Can Get Tangled

I had chartered the entire head-boat for a day of fishing with our Adult Ministries and Men's Ministries friends from around the state. When the captain announced we could lower our lines, I watched amazed as almost sixty people lowered their hooks and lead to the bottom. Because the current was strong, it was not long before some of those lines were tangled around other lines. To make matters more complicated, when a fish was caught, sometimes even more lines were tangled together. It took real patience and understanding to keep tempers from flaring and angry words from being spoken.

The boat reminded me of the church, and the many years Susan and I have been pastoring. Just like that boat, the church has many people in it, and they are all trying to do what they feel the Lord has called them to do. Just like the boat, because of the attacks of the enemy, many times our lives can also become entangled. It can happen, especially, when one, or more, is fighting a real attack of the enemy. Those situations require patience and understanding on everyone's part, in order to untangle things and get everybody back to fishing for the Kingdom.

On the boat that day, the patience and understanding paid off, we caught a lot of fish, and had a great time together. When we allow the Holy Spirit to work out the tangles within the body of Christ, we will also find that we can enjoy catching a great number of souls for God's Kingdom, and we can have a wonderful time doing it.

Romans 12:18, "If it is possible, as far as it depends on you, live at peace with everyone."

Ants Can be a Real Problem

Things had been very busy, and I missed the early morning fishing trips in the small boat. It would be great to be out again. I pulled the cover off the boat and began to check things out for the trip the next morning. As I opened one of the compartment lids, I could not believe the number of large carpenter ants inside it. As I continued to check other areas of the boat, I realized that I would need to do something about the ants if I was to use the boat the next morning. Because I had been so busy, and had failed to pay attention to the boat, I now had a real mess to take care of.

How true that is in our lives as well. We can get so busy doing our "stuff," that our walk and relationship with God just seems to get put on hold. Our personal devotion is passed up or overlooked, our investment of time into the ministry of the Kingdom of God drops off, and even our attendance at the House of God gets replaced with things that seem to need our attention. Something happens, and we realize that the closeness and fellowship we once enjoyed with Christ is not there. In the place of our relationship with Christ, Satan has set up residence with things that we need to get rid of.

Just as I could not allow the ants to stay in the boat, there may be things in your life you cannot allow to remain. When was the last time you really allowed the Holy Spirit to take inventory of your life and your relationship with Christ?

Psalms 139:23, "Search me, O God, and know my heart: try me, and know my thoughts."

Let's Have a Great Time Fishing

The captain of the boat was giving some last minute instructions before we arrived at the first fishing spot of the day. He explained that the current was strong today, and we would need a heavy lead to keep our lines from being pulled along the bottom, and getting entangled with the person fishing next to us. He also explained that we were not to drop our lines until he gave the instructions to do so. This would help to prevent the lines from becoming intertwined with the boats propellers or anchor. His final instruction was that if we didn't recognize the fish species we caught, we should allow the mates to remove it from the line. Some fish are dangerous if handled improperly. He concluded by saying, "I hope you have a great time today." We each listened intently, and then tried to follow all the instructions of the captain.

I wonder why so many people have such a difficult time following the instructions God gives in His Word and not a boat captain. Just as the captain gave us instructions for our own good, so we would have an enjoyable day, God's instructions are designed so we will have life, and have it to the fullest possible measure. God's desire is that we walk in victory, not being pulled along by the current of this world. He wants us to allow Him to work in our lives to achieve His purpose. It is never the plan of God to prevent us from finding joy and fulfillment in this life, but only to keep us safe.

Jeremiah 29:11, "'For I know the plans I have for you,' declares the LORD, 'plans to prosper you and not to harm you, plans to give you hope and a future.'"

It Will Be Worth the Effort

I knew the 18' Bass Tracker boat was not new, but it was in really good shape to be seventeen years old. The gel-coat on the outside was still shining, the engine started right up, and the trailer it set on had no signs of corrosion. It was only after I got it home that I discovered almost none of the wiring or switches worked. Fortunately, I have worked on boats most of my life, so this would not be a major problem.

Like this boat, we often find Christians in our churches that are in the same situation. Their exterior may have a nice shine, they may be quick to step up and do whatever you ask of them, and they may not have any obvious corrosion from the world around them. It is only when you get better acquainted with them that you discover some problems that were not obvious at first glance. They may be carrying some serious baggage from a previous broken relationship, an old wound from a former church that was never taken care of, or an old addiction from their old life of sin that has not been truly crucified at the cross.

Just as the boat I purchased was worth the effort to correct the unseen wiring and switch problems, these hurting people who serve in our churches are worth the effort of the Holy Spirit and the Body of Christ to help them correct the problems in their lives. Who is that person in your church who just needs your love and support to correct some wiring difficulties in their life? God may want to use you to help make that happen.

Galatians 6:2, "Carry each other's burdens, and in this way you will fulfill the law of Christ."

Tighten the Connections First

The man I was purchasing the boat from said that everything worked, so I accepted his word. After getting it home, I started checking out all the switches and finally came to the two fish finders on the boat. I switched the first one on, but nothing happened. My first thought was that I would need to replace them, but I wanted to try something first. I checked the power source, and there were twelve volts where they needed to be. I checked the second one, getting the same results. I was disappointed, but I was not ready to give up just yet. I unplugged the power cable at the fish finder, cleaned the contacts, and pushed them slightly apart, hoping to get a better connection. When I plugged the power cord back in and hit the on button, I was thrilled to see the unit turn on, and begin to function properly. The same process soon had both units working.

There are times in our Christian walk that we seem to have lost the power, and lost the ability to serve the Lord effectively. We become disappointed or disillusioned and can sense the presence of God seemingly missing from our lives. Maybe the problem is that we need to tighten up the connection with the Power Source. When you clean the contact points, and tighten up the connection in your relationship with Christ, you will discover the presence of the Lord to be fresh and new in your life. Don't give up just because things don't seem to be working for you; do the maintenance required and you will find there is still life there after all.

Jeremiah 29:13, "You will seek me and find me, when you seek me with all your heart."

One Size Does Not Fit All

Because I have a real love for fishing, I am seldom using only one rod when fishing offshore. I usually set up one outfit with cut bait to fish for the grunts, dropping the bait to the bottom and putting the rod in a rod holder to make sure it is not pulled overboard. I will then set up the next rod for grouper, and lower the live bait to the bottom as well. I may even pull the large spinning outfit from the rack, put a cork on it, and put out a live bait behind the boat, hoping for a kingfish. Sometimes this can make for some really serious situations if more than one rod is hit at the same time. My wife will usually ask me, "Why do you fish with so many lines out," and my stock answer to her is, "You can't catch fish with the line in the boat".

That is a great spiritual truth for your life and mine, also. When we are trying to reach people for Christ, one method may not work every time, in every situation. You might need to bait your hook with different bait, fish it at a different depth, and make your presentation somewhat differently. When things get fast and furious, I can always hand one of the rods to someone while I keep fighting the other fish. If you find your current technique for reaching people for the Lord is not working well, set out a few more rods, try different bait, and give the Holy Spirit a chance to use a new approach. I may look awkward sometimes, but I do catch fish.

John 21:6, "He said, 'Throw your net on the right side of the boat, and you will find some.'"

Seas Two Feet or Less

There is a standing joke between my son, Kenny, and me. When I am going off shore, I usually tell him, "The seas are two feet or less." Of course, that is not always the case when we get out there. I have been out on days when there was literally not a ripple on the water. I have also been on the Gulf in five to seven foot seas as well. The conditions are subject to change just as quickly as the weather changes. The same is true in our lives. We can have a period when there is not a ripple in life, everything is going smoothly, and there are no problems or difficulties. Things can change in a very short period of time. From calm and smooth conditions, our lives can suddenly be thrown into turmoil, and complications that we never saw coming. You might receive a diagnosis from the doctor, a letter of divorce proceedings from a spouse, or suddenly you find your child is on drugs, or pregnant and unmarried. The seas of life are no longer "two feet or less." The calm of life has turned into a raging sea of pain and heartache.

This is the time we must put our trust and confidence in the Master of the winds, the waves, and the sea itself. Just as Jesus commanded the winds and waves to be still for the disciples, He can command the circumstances of your life. The conditions you are facing may not change right away, but Christ can instantly bring peace to your heart, as you put your trust in Him.

Mark 4:39, "He got up, rebuked the wind, and said to the waves, 'Quiet! Be still!' Then the wind died down, and it was completely calm."

That Thing Can Sink Your Boat

My friend, Cary, and his brother, had taken their small Jon boat out on the grass flats to do some trout fishing. The water was only three or four feet deep, but because the winds had come up some, they were now in a fairly heavy chop. They began to notice that the waves were splashing over the rear gunnels of the boat, and water was quickly accumulating in the bottom of their craft. Almost without warning, the back corner of the boat, where my friend was sitting, dipped under the water, and they were suddenly floundering in the water with the boat sliding beneath the surface. All their gear was being blown away by the wind, and the movement of the waves. They regained their footing in the shallow water and righted the boat, but it would take them some time to get back to shore.

How many times have we found that life can treat us the same way? The world around us can slowly work itself into our hearts, and we begin to take on its corruption in our spiritual lives. At first, it doesn't seem to be much of a problem, then, without warning, our boat is capsized and we are floundering. We might somehow regain our footing, but lose all the witness and testimony that we had. We find that regaining the confidence of those around us will take some time and a lot of work. How much better it would have been not to have put our lives in that situation that capsized our walk with God.

Psalms 119:10-11, "I seek you with all my heart; do not let me stray from your commands."

It Needs More than a Repair

The trolling motor on the used Bass Tracker I had just bought did not want to come on. I originally tried it, before I made the purchase, and it work fine, but, now, there was no response from the switch. Using my volt meter, I began to check to see if I could locate the problem. The battery was reading fine, and even the place where the trolling motor wire connected to the power panel was fine. When I took a reading at the switch in the foot control, I found there was no power there. Tracing the wire back, I found that a connection repair had been made a foot or so from the switch. Checking both sides of the connection, I found that power was not getting through the wire repair. Instead of replacing the wire, someone had only made a quick splice repair.

How easily we can find this happening in our own spiritual lives. We have taken our need, or situation, to the Lord in prayer, but because we were unwilling to allow the Holy Spirit to do a complete work, we just made a quick repair instead. Things seemed to go fine for a while, but now we find the power of God is not working as it should be. Could the problem be because we were satisfied to make a repair, instead of allowing the Holy Spirit to do a whole new wiring job in our life?

Replacing the wire would be the best cure for the trolling motor, and allowing the Holy Spirit to do a new work in our hearts will be the best cure for our lives as well.

Ephesians 4:24b, "Put on the new self, created to be like God in true righteousness and holiness."

You Knew Better Dummy!!

The sun was barely up, and something had hit the piece of cut bait hanging under the cork. The lite bait casting rod began to bend hard, and I set the hook. I didn't know what it was, but it was pulling hard on the lite rod. As the fish came into view, I was disappointed to see it was a saltwater cat fish, something I would not be keeping. The fish has three large spiny barbs, one on each side, and one on the top. I have handled many of these over the years, and I usually use a towel and pin the fish solidly before attempting to remove the hook. I was in a hurry to get the line back into the water, so I simply reached down with the pliers to pull the hook free. The fish twisted violently, and the pain I felt, as one of the barbs punctured my finger, was almost unbearable. I pulled my hand back quickly, but the wound and my whole finger was already throbbing. As I hurried to get some ice on my finger, I was muttering to myself, "You know better, dummy, you know better."

I wish I could say fishing is the only place that I make foolish decisions, even when I know better. Life choices may bring another kind of pain, and often will have farther reaching consequences. It really hurts when we have to admit, "I knew better." As I write this, my finger is still sore. Some lessons are very painful to learn. Thank God, His forgiveness is still available, if we ask, but the pain may linger for some time.

James 4:17, "If anyone, then, knows the good they ought to do and doesn't do it, it is sin for them."

Cheap or Easy May Not be Best

The rear seat on the bass boat seemed to be moving more than it should. As I pulled the carpet away from the mounting plate, it didn't take long to recognize the problem. Whoever installed it opted to use something other than stainless steel. Because it was wet so often, it had rusted out. If they had just thought about it and spent a little extra money, they could have used stainless steel and I would not be replacing it now.

Too many times in our lives, we opt to choose the easy way, or the cheap and less demanding way, to achieve what we want. We fail to look ahead and ask what will be the results of this choice down the road for me, or someone coming behind me. That date with a person who doesn't know the Lord, or that second look when we really didn't need the first. Often words we utter, or thoughts we allow to linger may seem trivial at the time. Like the person who installed the seat mount, his choice was going to ultimately cost someone, in this case me.

The enemy loves to push us into making quick and prayerless decisions. He knows when we do that, we, or someone else, will pay the price for our poor choice. Taking a few extra minutes, or even days, to think and pray through something, so we can know God's will, can make a real difference. The seat mount was an easy fix without much cost, but for a marriage, or a personal testimony, there may be no fix. Even if there is, the cost may be high.

Proverbs 12:15, "The way of fools seems right to them, but the wise listen to advice."

Are Things in the Right Place?

The fish finder on the boat I had purchased was working fine, at least as long as I was not moving very fast in the water. As soon as I put the boat on plane, the signal was lost. When I began looking for the problem, I found that whoever had installed the fish finder transducer on the rear of the boat had mounted it in the wrong place. Where it was located, it lost contact with the water as soon as the boat jumped up on plane.

The place we locate Christ in our life can also greatly determine our success or failure in this life. If He is not established on the throne of our lives, we will find that when the real difficulties and trials come our way, we have no clear direction from the Holy Spirit. We struggle with finding the mind and will of God, when our lives are directed and controlled by other influences, such as our career, a relationship, or even subtle distractions. It is only as Jesus is in the proper place in our hearts that we can get a true reading on the choices around us, and make the decisions God wants us to make.

It only took a few minutes to move the transducer to the proper location, so the fish finder worked properly. Just recognizing the problem, but being unwilling to make the change, would not have accomplished anything. The same is true concerning the place we give Christ in our lives. He will not usurp the throne from you. Moving Christ to the throne of your life will be the best decision you have ever made.

Psalms 7:7, "Let the assembled peoples gather around you, while you sit enthroned over them on high."

Is the Tongue Weight Wrong?

I could tell as I pulled the boat toward my house that the weight on the trailer tongue was too light. The boat was positioned too far back on the trailer, and it did not provide sufficient tongue weight for the trailer to pull safely. I would need to adjust the position of the boat on the trailer before I attempted to pull it very far, or at highway speeds. To move the boat forward on the trailer would mean removing the winch stand, and adjusting it forward about eight inches. It would also mean that the carpeted bunks the boat rode on would need to be moved forward eight inches, also. The work took some effort, but the small adjustment proved to be just what was needed for the trailer to perform well.

I was willing to take some time, and make an effort to adjust the position of the boat on the trailer, but am I as quick to make the adjustments necessary in my walk with God? I was not content with the way the trailer pulled, but sometimes I remain content with the fact that my walk with Christ is not what it should be. I knew the unsafe situation the position of the boat on the trailer created, but I often fail to accept the spiritual danger I place my walk with Christ in by failing to make the changes necessary in my spiritual life.

I could feel the movement of the trailer, and knew I needed to make the adjustments. God is faithful to let us know when we need a spiritual adjustment, so let's be quick to make those adjustments as well.

Psalms 33:18, "But the eyes of the LORD are on those who fear Him."

It Pays To Know Your Fish

Bill, a missionary friend, had caught a couple of fish a few days before, and was asking what kind they were. He was new to our area, and was not yet acquainted with our local array. He had a brochure with pictures of different species, and thought the fish he had caught might be a bonefish or baby tarpon. I told him it was probably not bonefish in this area of the Gulf, but they might be small tarpon. When he showed me the pictures he had taken of the fish, I had to smile. The fish he caught were "lady fish," often called a "Poor Man's Tarpon," because they will jump when hooked.

How many Christians have found themselves deceived by the enemy, because they were not sufficiently aware of his schemes. He has a knack for making one thing look like something else, and we can be fooled into thinking something that is wrong is really OK. That relationship that seems to be an opportunity to help someone, suddenly turns into another thing entirely. The "prayer request" you shared about someone can be used as a means of bringing great pain to them. The mistaken identity of the fish Bill caught wasn't a big problem, but if we allow ourselves to be caught up in deception by the enemy, it can bring disastrous results. What you don't know can hurt you.

As Bill continues to fish our area, he will become more knowledgeable of what the fish are he is catching. As we grow in the Lord, we also need to become more aware of the deceptions of the enemy.

2 Corinthians 2:11, "Lest Satan should get an advantage of us: for we are not ignorant of his devices." KJV

The Bait Doesn't Catch Fish

The experiences that I have been privileged to enjoy through the years as I've been fishing have served to teach me many important lessons in my spiritual life. Recently, as I was considering the conflicts the church is going through, as we see changes in our service styles, our music styles, and many other facets of what we call church, I felt the Lord taking me back to a lesson from my days of fishing. We often remark that we use bait to catch fish. I suppose in one sense that might be partially true. However, the real truth is that bait does not "catch" fish, it only "attracts" fish to a hook the bait is attached to. The more attractive the bait is to the fish we are seeking to catch, the better opportunity we have for success.

We need to understand that the flashing lights we see in many services, the smoke some are using, and even the changing worship styles in our churches, are only the bait designed to attract the fish. They are not, and will never be the hook that catches the fish. The Gospel of Jesus Christ is the only means available to truly catch people for God. It is the spiritual hook that penetrates a heart, and brings the radical transformation necessary to give eternal life.

To be effective in fishing, we may need to use many different kinds of bait, but one part of successful fishing never changes, "You need a strong sharp hook." Let's not complain about the bait, or its presentation style, but remain thankful that the hook can still be a part of the presentation.

1Corinthians 9:22b, "I have become all things to all people, so by all possible means I might save some."

Stand Your Ground and Fish

The fishing location I had been given by a friend was one he had seen a head-boat on. This usually means it is a large reef, or area with a hard bottom, and would be good fishing. I positioned the boat over the location, and let the anchor rope come tight. We dropped our lines, and were soon reeling in fish. We had only been anchored about an hour, when a large head-boat was approaching our area. Instead of moving off his course to go around us, he continued to move in our direction. As he got "really close," he must have realized we were anchored in the very spot he was coming to. Instead of just moving away, he made a couple of hard circles around us causing the water to get pretty rough. He finally turned, and moved a few hundred yards away from us.

The enemy is never happy when you move in on what he assumes is his territory. Reaching out to someone with the love of Christ will quickly bring the anger of the enemy against you. I had as much right to be in that location on the water as the head-boat, so I just rode out the rough water he caused and remained at anchor, catching fish.

The enemy has no right, or authority, to push you away from what God wants you to do within His Kingdom. Don't let the angry boat captain, or a little rough water drive you away from where God has placed you. Your boat is anchored in Christ, and cannot be moved by the threats of the enemy.

Titus 2:15, "These then, are the things you should teach. Encourage and rebuke with all authority. Do not let anyone despise you."

Louder Does Not Mean Better

I had heard the new four stroke outboards were quiet, but I had not really been around them. As we climbed aboard the 32' center console, I noticed it had two of the new 275 HP Mercury four stokes on the back. I watched as the captain reached over, and turned the ignition of the first engine and then the second. I wondered if something was wrong, because I did not hear the customary sounds of the engines starting. He seemed to be unconcerned, so I looked back to see what was going on. To my surprise, both engines were running. We eased away from the dock. When we reached the open water, the captain told us to hold on to something as he pressed the twin throttle levers forward. The 32' boat literally seemed to leap out of the water as the twin 275's came alive with power.

There are those in the Kingdom of God whose lives seldom make much noise, and, in fact, it may seem there is no real power operating in their life. Don't be fooled by their quite demeanor. Many times, like those outboards, there may be little outward evidence of the power that is waiting to be unleashed. That quiet, unassuming person may go completely unnoticed in our church, or the work-place. Then the Lord shoves the throttle forward, and unleashes the power of the Holy Spirit that is in his/her life.

The Holy Spirit, Who equips and empowers our lives, does not need to make a lot of noise to have His power available for us.

1Corinthians 4: 19, "But I will come to you shortly, if the Lord will, and will know, not the speech of them which are puffed up, but the power."

Keep the Safety Gear Ready

Boat owners know there are regulations that require certain safety equipment to be on the boat at all times. You need to have on board such things as a paddle, flares, a fire extinguisher, and life jackets for each person. I have owned and operated a boat for almost fifty years, and to this day, I have never had an emergency where I needed to utilize all that safety equipment that the regulations require; not even the life jackets. I could easily respond, when told I must have them, "I never needed them before, so why are they required?"

How many times we display the same attitude with the regulations in the Word of God, even when we may not verbalize it. Scripture tells us repeatedly the value of knowing and obeying the regulations found in the Bible, but we often don't take the time or make the effort to read and study the Word. When you are faced with an emergency on a boat, it is easy to recognize why all that safety equipment is required. There are times that knowing and utilizing the promises of God would mean the difference in gaining victory or facing defeat. God's Word was not given to us so we would just have another book to read.

Just as the safety equipment for a boat is necessary for a safe day on the water, the Word hidden in our hearts is necessary so we can enjoy a safe and productive life in Christ.

Hebrews 4:12, "For the word of God is alive and active. sharper than any double-edged sword, it penetrates even to dividing of soul and spirit, joints and marrow; it judges the thoughts and attitudes of the heart."

Satan's Teaser is Not Funny

Those who have watched fishing programs, or had the opportunity to go offshore and fish for billfish or similar species, may have heard the term, "Teaser." A teaser is artificial bait deployed to attract your targeted fish close to the boat. It often has no hooks, and is kept just out of reach of the fish you are luring closer and closer to the boat. When the fish is within range, and in a frenzy to eat, a lure with hooks will be cast by someone in the fishing party. The targeted fish, by this time, has been working hard to catch the teaser, and when the new lure is presented, it quickly strikes the freshly offered bait with the hooks.

The enemy is a master teaser. He knows just what kind of desires are lurking in our hearts, and he deploys a teaser to begin attracting us closer. The teaser he uses may not be harmful within itself. It may not have any dangerous hooks, but, as we blindly follow the enticement created, we are lured ever closer to a waiting bait. The teaser of the enemy can be found in relationships, the desire to be more successful, a longing for the "good things" in this life, or you can fill in your own blank. Even if the teaser itself has no real sinfulness, or hooks attached, we need to be aware that the enemy can use many different things to lure us to within casting distance. Then he deploys something that we may reach out after, without realizing there are dangerous hooks attached to that bait. Many a billfish has fallen prey to a teaser.

James 1:14, "But every man is tempted, when he is drawn away of his own lust, and enticed."

Know the Signs of Transom Rot

For many years, the transom of a boat was constructed of wood, then fiber glassed over and gel coated. The wood gave structural strength to the transom, and provided a very good support for the motor to be mounted on. If the outboard mounting bolts were not sealed properly, though, water would leak into the wood area and rot would begin in the transom. Because the rot was concealed by the fiber glass covering, the damage might not be detected until there was a major structure failure in the transom. If repair was possible, it was usually very difficult and expensive. Many a boat has been discarded because of transom rot and failure.

The enemy loves to take advantage of small openings, or breaks in our spiritual armor and relationship with Christ, where he can begin to cause spiritual rot. He may use an unsaved friend whose beliefs can slowly pull us away from what we know is the truth; or it may be what we watch on TV, how we use our cell phones, or lies that seemed small at the time, but have escalated as we have tried to cover up poor choices. The enemy only needs a small place to enter in. He will then begin to bring rot and decay to that area, and it will spread until it causes great damage.

The only real cure for a rotten transom is to scrape away all the rotted area and replace it with new wood. Thank God, His love and mercy is more than sufficient to restore everything the enemy has destroyed in our lives!

Ephesians 6:13, "Therefore, put on the full armor of God, so that when the day of evil comes, you may be able to stand your ground."

Keep a Sharp Eye on the Gulls

I am always amazed, when we are fishing offshore, how quickly the sea gulls will locate us. All that is needed is for someone to catch a fish, or throw a fish or piece of bait into the water. Before long, the gulls are even trying to get the bait off your hook as you are casting your line out to fish. Sometimes the fellows with me think it is enjoyable to watch the birds dive for the scraps thrown overboard. I tell them right away, however, "If you continue to feed them, they will become a real nuisance, and you won't be able to get rid of them."

That statement is just as true concerning our lives and our walk with Christ. It seems that as soon as we come to know the Lord, the scavengers of this world show up. They want to steal whatever they can get from us. They will rob you of all that your new relationship in Christ has given you, taking it a little piece at the time. Just like with the birds, it may not seem like such a big deal at first, but if you allow them to begin to feed off you, you will find it difficult to get rid of them.

The birds will continue to get bolder and, until they end up landing on the boat, trying to get something from us. Zero tolerance is the only approach to take with the birds of this world who are trying to steal the blessings that God has given to you. Giving up a little bit here and there to appease is most certainly a recipe for disaster.

Ephesians 4:27, "Do not give the devil a foothold."

2 Corinthians 2:11, "In order that Satan might not outwit us. For we are not unaware of his schemes."

Forbidden Treasure or a Curse?

For my six-year-old grandsons, getting in the used 26-foot cabin cruiser was at the top of their to do list. They had been warned not to climb into the boat, and the ladder that gave access was raised hopefully beyond their reach just to make sure. Before their mom and dad got up the next morning, the resourceful duo was out of the house and soon climbing into the excitement of forbidden territory. When mom and dad got up a little later, they began searching to find the missing boys. After some time, they were located in the cabin of the boat. They had somehow locked the door, but were unable to get it unlocked. The fun and excitement they had anticipated quickly turned to fear, and was followed by some strong disciplinary action.

More than one child of God has been lured by the enemy to go someplace, or do something, they had been warned against. The devil has a way of lying to us, and convincing us the thrill and excitement will be worth the disobedience and possible consequences. Sometimes, it is too late to turn back when you find you are trapped in a bad situation, or a problem you can't seem to get out of. Their parents, fortunately for the boys, came looking for them right away and found them before they were injured. God will also come looking for us, but He may not always arrive in time to prevent us from suffering the consequences and pain. I'm sure those boys will think twice before climbing into that boat again. The lesson was learned, but at a price.

Romans 6:12, "Therefore, do not let sin reign in your mortal body so that you obey its evil desires."

Water in the Bilge is an Issue

The used Tracker boat I had purchased seemed to be running and working fine, but I noticed it was accumulating water in the bilge area when I was fishing. I could pump it out with the bilge pump, but, before long, there would be more water. It only seemed to be coming in while the boat was underway, not while I was sitting still, which confused me. After fishing one day, I decided to take a look at it when I got it home. I began by checking the bait well pumps and the transom plug, but found no reason for the water. Then I looked back at the engine, and saw a small tube running from it through the transom. When I looked inside to where the tube was going, I realized that it was the water pickup tube for the old style speedometer. I had rewired the boat, removing the tube from the dash area, just cutting it off in the rear of the boat. Every time the boat was underway, water was forced in through the tube and into the bilge.

Satan loves to create havoc in our walk with Christ by finding an opening in our old life to defeat us. He is very adept at seeking out those things you may have forgotten about, but that left an opening in your spiritual armor. It may have seemed a small issue then, but left open to the enemy, it can quickly become a major problem.

I plugged the line, and solved my water problem. Satan only needs a foot in the door. Ask the Holy Spirit to help you deal with that old issue, before it becomes much more serious.

Song of Solomon 2:15, “Catch for us the foxes, the little foxes that ruin the vineyards.”

Don't Assume it Will be Okay

Susan's brother had given us the 26' Bayliner, but it was 300 miles away. When we arrived with Danny's truck to tow it home, I noticed the tires were in bad condition. In fact, on two of the four tires, the tread was pulling away. We took time to pray before we left, but as we were going down the road, I questioned the wisdom of this decision. We had no spare, and the weight of the boat required all four tires for us to trailer it safely. If we had a flat, we would need to park the boat beside the road, try to find a tire that fit, and, even then, we didn't have a jack with us that would lift the trailer so we could change the tire.

Before you shake your head and ask why we would do something that foolish, make sure you can honestly say you have never done anything in your own life, especially you spiritual life, that lacked good wisdom. The situation with the trailer could have been a problem, but I have met people, in my 32 years of pastoring, who made choices that made that decision look brilliant. Men who convinced themselves that talking about personal things to that female on the job didn't mean anything. Women who dressed in a way that was very provocative, but excused it because it was in style. Teenagers who have gotten involved in premarital sex, but didn't see a problem because others were doing it.

Thank God, we made it back safely, but we cannot count on God always bailing us out of foolish decisions.

Proverbs 3:21, "My son, do not let wisdom and understanding out of your sight, preserve sound judgment and discretion."

Complaining Can Hide the Cure

My grandson, Kevin, and his wife were joining Susan and me for a day at the Anclote sandbar. Before I backed the center console into the water, I pushed the trim button on the motor to lower the outboard. Something was wrong; the trim on the motor did not come on, so I could not lower the engine. I tried several times, and finally told the others the trim was not working so we would have to postpone our day on the water. While I was grumbling to myself, and preparing to go back home, Susan asked me if we could use the smaller Bass Tracker to get to the sandbar. Why had I not thought of that? I was so busy grumbling about not being able to use the big boat, that I had completely forgotten about the Tracker.

Many times we have allowed something that seemed to be going wrong to get us into a mindset of grumbling and complaining. Instead, we should trust God to see if there was another option He was pointing us toward. Sometimes, we can miss what God has for us, because we fail to trust Him to work things out in such a way that it will be best for us.

It took only a few minute to go home, and come back to the ramp with the other boat. The fun day, that could have been ruined because of my grumbling and complaining, turned out to be a great time with the grandkids.

Let's stop complaining about what is going wrong, and look for what God wants you to see in the situation.

Romans. 8:28, "And we know that in all things God works for the good of those who love him, who have been called according to his purpose."

Expand Your Fishing Range

Many of the boats that have a center console also have a T-top that provides a shade or covering over it. Many T-tops are equipped with rod holders, attached to the back portion of the top, for holding fishing rods. These rod holders can be used to hold rods when running to your fishing area. They can also be used to place rods in when you want to fish behind the boat some distance, and be able to fish close to the boat, as well. This allows you to cover a larger area of the water more effectively. Missionaries are much like these rod holders on the T-top. They give the church an opportunity to reach out much further than would otherwise be possible. They can work to share the Gospel to foreign lands, and touch lives not normally possible for the local church.

Just as the rod holders on the T-top need the boat to be the platform base that supports them, the missionaries need the local church to be their support base. They cannot effectively do what God has called them to do without the financial support and the prayers that the church provides. Just as the rods in the T-top depend on the structure and support of the boat holding them up, the missionaries around the world depend on the local church to provide the support base for them.

Want to reach the fish that may be just beyond the reach of the rod you are holding? Try putting a rod in the T-top, support missionaries, and give yourself a chance to reach further out into the world.

Mark 16:15, "He said to them, "Go into all the world and preach the gospel to all creation."

The Sandbar is Ever Changing

The sand bar north of Anclote Island is a place Susan and I love to visit. The water surrounding it is very shallow, and the Gulf side has little or no sea grass on the bottom. You can walk several hundred yards on nothing but white sand. The size and shape of the bar is constantly changing, as the tide comes in and out throughout the day. On occasion, there is a large area above the water, and, at other times, the area above the water is very small. What is really amazing is how much it can change when rough weather or a storm comes through the area. There have been times when we have returned to the sand bar after rough weather, and hardly recognized the shape of it. Even with the constant change to the sand bar, the beauty and allurement remains.

Daily living has a way of bringing us constant change, just as the water and weather is constantly changing the sand bar. Problems and difficult situations in life can be like the tide, constantly rising and falling to cover or expose our fears and failures. The same can be true of the rough weather or storms that buffet us from time to time. Just when you think you know what you are doing, and what God has planned for your life, a strong storm comes along and nothing looks the same anymore.

Don't give up. Even when things don't always remain the same, the sand bar is still there, and it still attracts many visitors because of its beauty. Your beauty will be seen in your steadfastness.

Psalms 121:3, "He will not let your foot slip; He who watches over you will not slumber."

Crab Traps Require Vigilance

If you have been out on salt water, you have seen the small Styrofoam balls dotting the waterways. Compared to its surroundings, the small buoy seems insignificant. In fact, you may get careless and not notice the buoy as you are approaching it. This is especially true if you are running at night, and do not have a good light to illuminate your way. The buoy would not present any problem if it was not for what it is attached to. The buoy is attached to a rope, and the other end of the rope is attached to a crab or fish trap lying on the bottom. If you run over one of these buoys, the propeller can grab the rope and pull the attached trap very quickly to your motor. When this happens, your engine can stall, and even be damaged by the force of the trap hitting the engine. It can be a real problem untangling the rope, and trap from your engine and propeller.

There are spiritual traps in life that line the path that has been laid out for us. God, through His word, has made us aware of them with spiritual marker buoys. Just like many boaters, we find we are often paying little attention to our surroundings. Perhaps, we have stepped out of the light of His will, and do not see the marker buoys. Our first hint that something may be wrong is when the power of God in our life has stalled, and we find our life is all tangled up in the enemy's trap. If only we had just been watching for the buoys!

1 Peter 5:8, "Be alert and of sober mind. Your enemy, the devil, prowls around like a roaring lion looking for someone to devour."

The Stinger Hook Can Hurt, Too

When I fish the grass flats, I often place a live bait under a cork, because there is a good chance I will catch a shark. With live bait, I usually place the hook close to the head, because most predator fish will hit the bait head first in order to swallow the small fish without encountering the sharp fins on its back. A shark does not need to hit the bait from the head, so he will often bite off a portion of the bait if it is too large to swallow completely. To make sure I don't miss the shark, I place a "stinger" hook in the tail of the bait that is attached to the primary hook. When the shark grabs just the tail portion of the fish, he finds my stinger hook.

Sometimes, as believers, we are deceived into thinking that as long as we are not really "involved" in a particular sin, a little flirting around with it is not a danger. We need to know that the enemy is a master at using stinger hooks to catch you and me unaware when we continue to flirt around an area of sin.

My stinger hook is usually smaller than the hook in the head, but it is securely fastened to the primary hook. I will have a good chance of catching any predator that misses the first hook by biting short.

Don't be deceived into believing there is no danger in what you are doing. It may be just that the stinger hook is small and cleverly hidden in the bait. You may never see the danger until Satan sets the hook.

Proverbs 4:26, "Give careful thought to the paths for your feet, and be steadfast in all your ways."

What are the Fish Feeding On?

If you want to be successful in fishing, it is important that you know what your targeted fish is feeding on. I will often take the first targeted fish I catch, and cut it open to see what is in its stomach. This will tell me very quickly what he has been feeding on. If he has been eating that kind of food, so will the others. It is definitely a waste of time to offer a fish something that he is not interested in or attracted to.

It is a fundamental truth of which the enemy of our soul is also aware. When he sets out to tempt you and me, he specifically uses those things that he knows have either been a part of our past, or still remain a desire in our heart. He then tailors the bait to specifically target our weakness. He will continue to use those things, until we recognize that the only way we can overcome that temptation is to eliminate the weakness from our lives. That is only possible as we learn to surrender those desires into the control of the Holy Spirit, and allow Him to replace them with desires the enemy cannot use against us.

If you are wondering why you seem to face the same temptations over and over, again, maybe the enemy has taken a look inside your heart and figured out what kind of bait you have been feeding on. If you allow the Holy Spirit to help you change your diet, you will find there is freedom from those continuing temptations.

James 1:14-15a, "But each person is tempted when they are dragged away by their own evil desire and enticed. Then, after desire has conceived, it gives birth to sin."

Just Get the Bait in the Water

One of the reasons I love to fish in salt water is the amazing variety of fish there. You can find fish that swim very slowly, to the Wahoo that swims up to 60 MPH. There are fish that are drab earth tone colors, and others that have every color in the rainbow. There are fish so small that you would never see them with the naked eye, all the way to the fish that weighs tons. Some fish make noises when they are caught, some change color when they are removed from the water, and many have mechanisms in place that are highly poisonous for protection. Putting your bait in the water gives you an opportunity to catch so many varieties of fish that there is always excitement when you are reeling in the line. Some fishermen target particular species of fish, but most of us just drop our bait in the water looking for the excitement of the catch.

When you share the Gospel of Jesus Christ, it is much like the fishing that is experienced in salt water. The world around us provides us with people that are as varied as the fish in the water. They are coming from many backgrounds, circumstances, situations, and cultures, so you never know who the Gospel might catch. There are some within the church who are good at targeting certain groups of people, but many others of us just put the bait over the side and get excited about the opportunity to catch someone for Christ. Let me encourage you, whether you are targeting fish, or just hoping to catch something, get the bait in the water.

Luke 5:10b, "Then Jesus said to Simon, 'Don't be afraid; from now on you will fish for people.'"

Patience Can Change the Result

The rod tip dipped sharply and I reeled as hard as I could, but I was not quick enough. The large grouper I had hooked dove back into the rock hole, and wedged his body in tightly. I pulled hard a couple of times, but he would not budge. I knew he was still there, but unless he came out of the hole on his own, I would not be able to get him. I disengaged the spool on the reel and set the clicker, giving the fish a few feet of slack and waited. I kept a close eye on the rod, and it only took a few minutes before I heard the clicker go off on the reel. In one motion, I engaged the spool, and reeled as hard as I could, lifting the rod tip sharply. This time, I won the battle, and the large grouper was soon in the fish box.

Sometimes we can find that those we are trying to reach for Christ just seem to pull away from us. They wedge themselves into a defensive attitude, and become very resistant to any pulling and tugging we might do. Let me encourage you to disengage the spool, set the clicker, and give them some slack. Wait patiently, and through prayer, be sensitive, as you keep an eye on things. The Holy Spirit can convince them to change their mind, and offer you a second opportunity to reach them for Christ.

Don't be afraid to back off some. Just as I knew the grouper was still hooked, you can be assured God will not allow your words to be lost on them.

Ephesians 5:2a, "Walk in the way of love, just as Christ loved us and gave Himself up for us."

Stay Current with the Rules

Dan brought the fish into the boat, and asked me what kind it was. I looked over at it, but was not certain. Because many of the salt water fish are regulated, it is very important to know what you are keeping, and also what the regulations for them are. I usually have an up-to-date FWC magazine in the boat for whenever there is a question. The magazine not only tells the regulations for the most common fish, but even has a full color picture for good identification. After looking in the magazine, we determined it was a Lane Snapper and was large enough to keep.

The Word of God is the FWC magazine for our spiritual questions in life. When we are uncertain about a decision we need to make, or something we want to do, we can simply open the Word of God and find what the regulations are for that principal for our lives. God was good enough to put "word pictures" of people's lives, and even many incidents for us to compare with ours. David's adultery is a good picture of why we should never go there. Paul's decision to follow God's voice concerning the boat he was on not only saved his life but the lives of all the others.

The FWC officer seldom accepts ignorance for an excuse for an undersized fish. We will also find there are always consequences when we choose to go against what the Word of God gives as regulations for our lives. When you are not sure about a fish, the FWC magazine is a great help. When you are not sure about a spiritual question, check God's Word.

James 1:5a, "If any of you lacks wisdom, you should ask God."

Let God Deal with the Mess

It would be Kenny's first fishing trip with us on his brand new boat. Because Troy was familiar with how we fish, and some of the other aspects of what we would do, I asked him to ride with Kenny. We stopped on the first number and immediately the six men in Kenny's boat were hooked up, and fish were coming in the boat quickly. They were catching so many that Troy told them to just throw the fish in the bottom of the boat, and he would get them on ice later. Within an hour, the clean, shiny new boat was littered with fish, fish scales, and bloody water. Kenny looked around, and I could see the panic on his face. Apparently, Troy saw it, too. He picked up an empty five gallon bucket, filled it with water from the Gulf, and splashed it over the interior of the boat. He then calmly looked over at Kenny, and said, "That should do it."

If you have been a part of a busy church for any time, you know that doing ministry, and especially reaching out to the lost, can sometimes get a little "messy." Those who are coming to the Lord are far from perfect, and they have not yet become accustomed to all of our church norms. Don't panic...be patient. Allow God to handle the messes. He has a great way of not being too concerned about the "mess," but being focused on reaching the lost. If it gets too messy, He will splash some water of the Holy Spirit on it. Our job is to keep on bringing fish into the boat.

Luke 19:10, "For the Son of man is come to seek and to save that which was lost."

Follow the Breadcrumb Trail

My old Lawrence 1600 GPS has a feature not found on all the newer GPSs. It draws a dotted line, called a breadcrumb trail, from where you are to the location you have punched in. This allows you to navigate to your location without worrying about staying on a specific compass heading, just follow the breadcrumb trail. As simple as that may sound, when I have someone inexperienced driving the boat, while I am in the back cleaning fish, they often get off course. I am usually focused on cleaning the fish, and I can't always tell that we are getting off course. When I look back at the wake and see a big curve instead of a straight line, I know that the driver has gotten off the breadcrumb trail. I can get them back on track by re-plotting from the current position, and the GPS will draw another trail from that position to our destination.

As believers, trying to follow the will of God, there are times we lose sight of that will and get off course. The Holy Spirit will quickly let us know, and He will re-plot the course again, if we let Him. We may have lost some time, and had to dodge a few extra obstacles, but He can get us back on track and following God's will again.

If you get your life off the "breadcrumb trail" that God has drawn for you, it does not mean He no longer cares. He just needs you to allow Him to re-plot the course and get you back on track.

Jeremiah 10:23 LORD, "I know that people's lives are not their own; it is not for them to direct their steps."

Be Patient with the Young One

The steering on Troy's boat had gone out, and we were fifteen miles from the dock. My oldest son, Kenny, was with us, so he tied a rope off from his boat's stern to the bow cleat on Troy's boat and began the slow ride in. Things were going well, until we came to the channel leading into Cedar Key. It had been a long trip, and Kenny had almost forgotten about Troy's boat behind him. As he approached one of the sharp turns in the channel, he failed to swing wide enough for Troy's boat to clear the buoy. Suddenly, Troy was yelling for Kenny to stop. Thankfully, he was heard, and with an adjustment in his track, Kenny had things in control again.

Sometimes, we find ourselves facing the same kind of situation when we attempt to provide spiritual guidance for a new convert who has little understanding about what living for Christ means. We can be just moving along in a normal routine for us, unaware that the one following us has no idea what is going on or why. When they begin to loudly protest what you are doing, it can be easy to become impatient with them. Just as Troy and his boat were at the mercy of Kenny pulling him, that new child of God is at our mercy as well. The turns and maneuvers may seem simple to us, but it may not allow for their immaturity.

It's a great privilege to disciple someone who is new in Christ, but recognize they may not be up to the difficult turns you are making.

Matthew 19:14, "Jesus said, 'Let the little children come to me, and do not hinder them, for the kingdom of heaven belongs to such as these.'"

A Day Can Change Everything

It's not often that I am blessed to fish two days in a row. I was excited about the trip planned on my boat for Friday, and the trip on the head boat, Saturday, with Finish Strong Ministries. Friday dawned with absolutely perfect weather. When we left the last channel marker and pointed the bow west, the water was almost flat calm. The entire day saw the weather remain calm and beautiful.

When we arrived at the head boat, Saturday, it was a different story. The wind was already blowing fifteen to twenty miles per hour, and the forecast said it would not get much better. Thank God, the head boat was a twin hull catamaran, about eighty-five feet long, and could handle the four foot seas.

It's amazing what a difference a day can make in the weather and in our lives. We have all been blessed with those times when it seemed that every blessing God has available was coming our direction. There are also other days, when it seems that God may have forgotten you, or, at least, ran out of blessings for you. Instead of letting the enemy bring fear or doubt, know that on those days the hand of God will provide you with everything you need to ride out the difficulties you face. It is often in those times when we can experience the presence of the Lord in a special way. The outcome of a stormy day is not decided by the winds and seas, as they attempt to capsize your vessel, but it will be determined by your faith in Christ.

Mark 4:39, "He got up, rebuked the wind, and said to the waves, 'Quiet! Be still!' Then the wind died down, and it was completely calm."

Look Beyond the Empty Spool

The drag on the Penn rod and reel I had set out began to scream. I pulled the rod from the holder, and applied pressure to the fish. This was the second large king fish I had hooked, so I asked the mate to get Mark, a missionary friend, to come over so he could fight the fish. As Mark took the rod, the fish made a mad dash for freedom, peeling the line off the reel. I watched frantically, wondering if it would spool the reel and break the line. I couldn't believe my eyes when the end of the line and the knot I had used to tie it to the spool was within sight. I just knew if the fish made one final lunge it would break the line.

Sometimes, we may wonder if that friend or family member who has been running from the Lord has reached a place where there is no hope of them coming to Christ. You have prayed and fasted, and it looks like the line has run out. One more pull, and they will be gone. Now is the time to really believe God to work the miraculous. God can do what seems to be impossible, even when there seems to be no hope.

The mate on the boat suddenly took the rod from Mark, moved quickly to the other side of the boat, and began to retrieve some of the line to the spool. He then handed the rod back to Mark, who ultimately was able to bring the fish close enough to the boat that it could be gaffed and landed.

2Peter 3:9b, "God is patient with you, not wanting anyone to perish, but everyone to come to repentance."

Finding Value in the Lost

It was our first full day in El Salvador, and Susan and I were scheduled to meet our host, and his wife, at 10 A.M. for breakfast. As Susan and I left the apartment to walk down the steep incline to the cafeteria, I noticed a 19' boat off to the side with a dirty tattered tarp attempting to cover it. It was obvious from the tires sunk in the dirt, and the weeds growing around it, that it had been that way a long time. When I asked our host about it, he was not really aware of it being there. It was my love for boats that had drawn my attention to something that had little value to him.

The same is often true when we are around those who do not know the Lord. If our heart holds little value for the lost, we can often walk by them, or even live next door to them, and never really be aware of their lost condition.

The condition of the boat was not the reason our host was unaware of its presence; it was the fact that boats had little value to him. When you and I truly value the souls of those around us, we will be drawn to them no matter what they may look like. That kind of value will only come through a true work of the Holy Spirit in our hearts.

We must place great value on the lost...Jesus died for them. You will be amazed how many you will begin to "see" along the path of life, as we ask God to help us take notice.

John 3:16, "For God so loved the world that He gave His one and only Son, that whoever believes in Him shall not perish, but have eternal life."

He Can Make Heavy Seas Also

The weather report had not prepared us for what we encountered, as we idled past the Sand Key Bridge in the early morning darkness. The swells coming in from the Gulf were already 3-4 feet. I cautiously turned the boat around and anchored at the bridge, hoping the weather would get better. As we waited, we watched as boat after boat went past us only to turn around and come back in. An hour later, we were back at the dock, loading the boat on the trailer. A man, launching his boat, asked why we came back in so early. I told him about the rough water, and he remarked, "We are heading to the Middle Grounds." I looked at the 21-foot boat he was launching, and said, "Not today you're not."

How many times have we, as believers, found the best laid plans we had devised were quickly going south on us. We had made all the preparations, maybe even believed we had heard from God, but it was all coming unglued now. The plans we had made that day seemed to be based on good information, but we quickly discovered that things can change. By coming back in, I would have the opportunity to go again another day.

Make sure the difficulties you are encountering are not God trying to tell you something. The devil is not the only one who can use circumstances to divert us from what we want to do. Before you blame the devil, ask God if the rough seas are His doing.

Acts 5:39, "But if it is from God, you will not be able to stop these men; you will only find yourselves fighting against God."

Fighting the Spiritual Red Tide

The Red Tide that develops along the Gulf coast of Florida can quickly affect the fish population. Called Red Tide because it is a red algae bloom, it affects the color of the water. It can spread rapidly, and it is dangerous to the fish population. It depletes the oxygen level in the water, causing the fish to suffocate and eventually die. When it is in high concentrations, you can see thousands of dead fish floating on the water in the area of the tide, washing up on the beaches. The smell can be terrible.

We can suffer a similar situation in our churches if we allow attitudes such as anger, bitterness, selfishness, and the like, to grow within the body. Like the Red Tide, these attitudes will quickly spread, and, if left unchecked, can choke the spiritual oxygen out of the congregation. Then, just as with the Red Tide, the casualties will begin to show up. You will find marriages suffering, or physical sickness will become more prevalent, and the division caused by the lack of spiritual oxygen will block any work of the Holy Spirit to reach the lost for Christ.

With Red Tide, you just have to let it run its course, but not so with the Red Tide in our churches. God's people must recognize the problem, and address it with prayer and submission to the Holy Spirit. Don't wait until the casualties begin floating around because of oxygen depletion before you address the spiritual Red Tide. The odor from these casualties can be just as bad as from the dying fish, and will keep people from seeking out your church.

Romans 12:9, "Love must be sincere. Hate what is evil; cling to what is good."

The Waves Can Get Bigger

As we cleared the inlet at Clearwater Pass, the wind from the north was creating two-foot waves. Because we were running south with the waves, the twenty-mile run would not be very rough. It wasn't long before we were anchored on our numbers and bringing fish aboard. The weather report said the 10-knot winds should diminish after lunch, but the weather man missed it again. In fact, the winds increased, and now the seas were 3-4 feet and still coming from the north. I knew the ride back to the dock would take much longer and not be nearly as smooth.

Many of the things God calls us to do in life can run into the same changing circumstances. When we first start, things seem to be going our way and the ride is fairly smooth and fulfilling. Just as the weather went south on us that day, the same call of God can begin to encounter rough weather and seas that are hitting you head on. You may find, as we did, that you are required to move a little slower, and watch the waves carefully.

Just remember this, the same God that was with you in the calm seas, when things were going well, is the same God who is with you in the rough seas. My boat rode very well in the 2-foot seas, but I knew it would also be safe in the four-foot seas.

God will get you to where He has called you to go... the trip may just be a little rougher than you anticipated. No matter how difficult the trip, God will see you through.

Psalms 54:4, "Surely God is my help; the Lord is the one who sustains me."

Watch Out for the Octopus

The rod Brandon was using showed that there was something on the line, but it was not the typical pull of a fish. As he brought it within sight, we were all amazed to see the 18" octopus caught by the hook. We took a couple of pictures, then I looked for a way to get it off the hook and let it go. I tried the de-hooker and shaking it off, but it would not come free. I finally took the filet knife and reached in to cut the hook free. As soon as I got close to the tentacles, they began to wrap around my arm and hand, and the suction cups on the tentacles were clinging to my skin.

Sometimes the choices or decisions we have made in life can offer the same kind of challenge when we try to get free of the results of those choices. No matter what we try, the tentacles of the enemy just seem to continue to wrap around our lives, and prevent us from finding the liberty we are seeking. As soon as I would peal one tentacle free, the octopus would just wrap another one around my arm again. It was not until I cut the hook loose that the octopus dropped back into the water.

You can be free from the clutches of your choices and decisions, but the process may take more than you first expect. Once the enemy has a hold on your life, he never surrenders easily. Freedom may require you to establish strong disciplines in your life to break loose from the suction cups of the enemy. Allow the Holy Spirit to guide you, because freedom is possible in Christ.

Galatians 5:1, "It is for freedom that Christ has set us free."

Be Mindful of the Time Invested

It was only a small wooden boat, and we moved it in the lakes and rivers with just two paddles. A little later in life, we were fortunate enough to have a 7 1/2 HP Johnson outboard, and I thought we really had it made. I remember fishing from that boat with cane poles we had bought from the tackle store, and I suppose it was in those early days that I acquired a love for fishing and being on the water. As special as that was, what was even more special were the times I had with my dad and two brothers. In our modern day, when we have iPhones, iPads, and i everything else, I wonder if children are growing up with any memories of special times spent with their Mom and Dad and siblings.

Those wonderful times that I spent with my Dad and siblings helped shape and define me as a person. They helped me to recognize the value of family and time spent together. Today, my sons have children of their own, and I believe the time I spent with them in their formative years also played a part in shaping their lives. I know I am proud of who they have become, and the kind of fathers they are.

Mom and Dad, don't allow some electronic device to be what will shape and define the lives of your children. You only have a few years to invest in their lives, and time invested now will pay big dividends later. Failure here can set in motion a chain of events that will prevent them from finding God's plan for their lives.

Proverbs 22:6, "Start children off on the way they should go, and even when they are old they will not turn from it."

Don't Give in to Bait Thieves

It was the third or fourth time I had felt something hit the bait, but now all was still. I reeled in the line and just as I thought, the bait thieves had worked their magic and cleaned the hooks. This was now being repeated too often, so I told the guys with me to reel in their lines and we would move to another spot. I had hope that it would be more productive. They had been experiencing the same kind of misfortune, so they were glad to comply.

There are times in our spiritual lives when we just need to recognize that the bait thieves, the lies and deception of the enemy, are robbing us of all God desires to do in our lives. Sometimes, we just need to make the decision that what we are doing is not working, and seek God as to what we really need to be doing.

We could have stayed where the bait thieves were taking all of our bait, but it made more sense to change locations, hoping for something better. Someone has said, "To continue to do the same thing and expect a different result is insanity." Staying in a place where you are making no spiritual gain, and not finding God's best for your life, is just as foolish as staying and letting the bait thieves steal your bait. Don't be content to allow the bait thieves of lies and deception to ruin your day. Pick up the anchor, and move to where God wants to richly bless your life.

The plan God has for you does not include wasting your life with bait thieves.

John 10:10, "The thief comes only to steal, kill, and destroy; I have come that they may have life, and have it to the full."

Success is Counted Together

I was watching a YouTube video showing a boat anchored near an offshore platform, and the men on board catching Mangrove Snapper. As I watched, something the men were doing caught my attention. The bow of the boat was toward the oil rig, so one man would stand in the bow, casting his bait toward the oil rig. When he hooked a fish, he would move toward the rear of the boat to bring the fish in. As soon as he moved, a second man would take his place, cast his bait in, and when he was hooked up, he would repeat the process. The cooperation and teamwork of the men were allowing all of them to catch fish without getting their lines tangled under the oil rig, or with each other.

That kind of cooperation is also vital in the church, if we are to be effective in the work of the Lord. There can be no place for selfish, self-centeredness, or the enemy will use that to keep us constantly tangled up with each other, and defeated by the obstacles we are facing.

The main object for the men on the boat was catching fish, not just see who could catch the most. The object of the Church is to win people for Christ, not see who will be first, or get the most recognition. We need to cheer on the success of others, even when things are not going all that well for us. We will then know we truly have a servant's heart for the Kingdom of God. It's more important that the Church reach people for Christ, not how many we catch personally.

Romans 12:10, "Be devoted to one another in love. Honor one another above yourselves."

Beware of the Short Fish

The line went tight, and I reacted quickly to set the hook. It took a few minutes, but finally I saw the color and knew it was a red grouper. It was large, but would it be large enough? I got it in the boat, took a picture, and then for the moment of truth...was it the twenty inches required by law for me to keep? We laid it on the measuring device, but no matter how hard we tried, it was just short of twenty inches. After several comments about grouper sandwiches, I threw it overboard to allow it to grow a little more.

Sometimes, in our walk with God, we want things to fall into the plan and will of God. We recognize that something is just not right. When we want something so badly, we may try to stretch the truth of God's word just a little so that what we have planned will fit. In our hearts, we know it isn't reaching His requirements for our lives.

When the comment about the grouper sandwich was made, I reminded them that the fine for keeping the short fish could buy many grouper sandwiches. When you and I stretch what we know to be the truth of God's word to fit our own wants and desires, we can bring more cost to our lives than we could have imagined.

Be careful to measure accurately what you are thinking of doing. Make sure you are not stretching the truth, so you can do something that God has not approved of in His Word. The cost of the sandwich will be more than you will want to pay!

Psalms 119:10, "I seek you with all my heart; do not let me stray from your commands."

Failure Does Not Mean Finished

We launched the boat, placed the gear on board, and were ready to head out to fish. Carey mentioned that the men in the boat next to us at the ramp could not get the motor started. I asked if they were having battery issues, but he said the owner had just installed two new batteries. They were reluctantly backing the trailer down to reload the boat. Whatever plans they had were now dissolving. They thought they had everything under control.

Each of us has found the same true, at one time or another. We went to God with a problem or situation, and after much prayer and confession, we believed the situation was defeated. However, we have an enemy who loves to lurk on the sidelines, and, at a time when we least expect it, he will launch an attack that blindsides us. That old craving, attitude, or anger we thought we had fixed seems to come rushing back at us with a vengeance. It is easy, at those times, to think that our prayer and confession did not work. Don't let the enemy lie to you! Pick yourself up, ask God to forgive you for letting down your guard, and keep your faith intact. Each of us have faced those times when we know the enemy got the best of us, but those who are growing in Christ will not allow that failure to define who they will be. Load the boat back on the trailer, and allow God to work you through this. Remind the enemy there will be another day and time, and he will not win!

Psalms 119:29, "Keep me from deceitful ways; be gracious to me and teach me your law."

The Value of Good Preparation

One thing you quickly discover, as you begin fishing offshore 15-20 miles, is that you cannot afford to forget to bring something with you that you might need. At that distance, you cannot just run back to shore and get any items you left behind. It is for that reason that I always use the day before my trip to prepare the boat, and get together everything I think I will need. I also check the batteries, the fuel level, life jackets, electronic equipment, anchors and line, and, of course, the rods and reels. The list is long, so I have actually put it on my computer so I can double check it. I know the value of being as prepared as possible before I leave home for my fishing trip offshore.

How sad if we do not see that same value before we leave our home, and head out into the hostile environment we call our job, our school, or any other place where we will encounter those who are not believers. It is not unusual to run into people who are angry, bitter, or just having a bad day. There are also those who are hurting from a broken marriage or other dysfunctional relationship, people who are being attacked by disease, or someone who has just given up on life.

On the Gulf, I want to be as ready as possible for any situation I might encounter. Jesus is calling us to be His hands and feet, His voice and heart, to a lost world. Taking time for prayer and the word of God, before we leave the dock of our home, is a great idea.

Matthew 10:16, "I am sending you out like sheep among wolves. Therefore be as shrewd as snakes and as innocent as doves."

Get Away From the Structure

We heard the large 30 to 50 pound Drum were biting under the Howard-Franklin Bridge, so Susan and the boys went with me to see what we could find. I knew they would be holding close to the bridge pilings, so I positioned the boat so we could easily move it away from the structure when the fish hit. I placed the bow of the boat so that it almost touched the bridge piling ledge, and allowed the boys to stand on the ledge with their rods. As soon as the fish hit, they would quickly step in the boat. I would allow the bow to move away from the pilings as they fought the fish. The only chance we had of landing such a large fish was to get it away from the structure.

We need to be aware of that same truth, as we attempt to disciple a new brother or sister in Christ. We have to find a way of moving them away from those situations and circumstances that have caused their detrimental lifestyle. We prayerfully move them into a place where the people of God, and the Spirit of God, can help them make the needed changes in their lives.

If we had not made the effort to move the fish away from the barnacle-encrusted pilings, they would have easily cut the line on the sharp edges and we would have lost them. Failing to get new believers away from the old friends and patterns of their former lives will almost always ensure a break-off. Ask the Holy Spirit to help you guide them away from the dangers that are present.

2 Corinthians 6:17, "'Therefore, come out from them and be separate,' says the Lord. 'Touch no unclean thing, and I will receive you.'"

Guarding Against Corrosion

Occasionally, I remove everything not fastened down on the boat and go through it. This includes the anchor, the rope, the spotlight, the safety kit, and the tool kit. Even though some of these, like the safety kit and tools, may not have even been used, I know the saltwater environment of fishing in the Gulf has a way of corroding and deteriorating them. Because they are not often used, it is easy to forget and neglect taking proper care of them. The metal in the tool kit is especially vulnerable to the salt air, and rust will quickly began to form if it is not taken care of. I usually clean and dry each piece. Before returning the kit to the boat, I spray it with an oil-based lubricant to help prevent corrosion.

Scripture says you and I are not of this world, but we do live in this world. For that reason, we are always subject to the corrosion that can come from the atmosphere of sin and evil that is constantly present around us. We can get very busy doing the work of the Lord, and forget proper maintenance. It is important that we regularly examine our spiritual life, and take any steps necessary to assure no corrosion is beginning to form. The Holy Spirit is well able to help us discover those areas where the atmosphere of this world is corroding our lives and some attention is needed. We need to ask the Holy Spirit to examine our hearts regularly, and allow Him to act before the corrosion forms.

Psalms 139:23-24, "Search me, God, and know my heart; test me and know my anxious thoughts. See if there is any offensive (corrosion) way in me, and lead me in the way everlasting."

Safety in the Marked Channel

The first GPS I owned did a great job of helping me locate my fishing spots, but it did not have a good map of the channels and buoys near shore. When it was dark or foggy, it was difficult to follow the channel, especially when there were sharp twists and turns. You only realized that you were moving out of the channel when the depth finder began to show that you were moving into shallow water, sometimes too late. The new GPSs have better mapping, and you can even purchase SD cards that have more mapping specifics on them. The one I have now shows, in white, the exact location of the channel and each of the marker buoys, their color, and number. No matter how dark or foggy it gets, all I have to do is keep the curser, which represents the boat, in the white area, and I am safely in the channel.

Life in a sinful world can also throw you some sharp dangerous curves and channel changes, and because of the darkness, the channel markers may not always be easy to distinguish. Sometimes, we may not realize that we are drifting out of the channel and into an unsafe area until it is too late. There is a better way than following your own lead. Allow the voice of the Holy Spirit to be your GPS (God Positioning System). He is that inner voice that comes, when we accept Christ, to map out a safe channel for us to follow. He will help you navigate, and stay in the safety of the channel of God's will for your life.

Psalms 25:5, "Guide me in Your truth and teach me, for You are God my Savior, and my hope is in You all day long."

Finding New Fishing Spots

I love the new technology that is available for boat owners and fishermen. The new GPS/Fish Finder combo I recently purchased has a great feature. When we are running to a destination, I keep a sharp eye on the depth finder. It shows the bottom we are passing over, and, if there is a drop-off or structure showing, it is a possibility that the fish are holding there. I used to have to turn around, and , hopefully, locate the area again. This is not always easy when you are running 35-45 MPH, and have gone some distance past it. With the new Track Back feature on the GPS, I can just move the cursor back to the location on the depth finder, and mark the new location. Now you have the coordinates, and can easily return to the spot.

There are times, in our spiritual lives, when we are moving in the direction God is leading, but an opportunity may present itself that is of great interest. We may move past it, and feel that the moment is lost. God often places opportunities in our path, as we walk in obedience. If we are sensitive, we can be in tune to what He might be saying to us. Allow the Holy Spirit a chance to guide you to that new place God has pointed out to you. Be quick to detect His signals, and you may just find out why He had you moving in a certain direction.

I have found some of my most productive fishing spots by keeping my eyes on the fish finder. Don't miss what God may have for you, because you allow the enemy to bring distractions.

Psalms 31:3, "Since You are my rock and my fortress, for the sake of Your name lead and guide me."

The Value of the Anchor Spot

As we pulled up to the spot marked by the GPS, I knew that it would be difficult to anchor exactly where we needed to, because the wind and the current were not moving in the same direction. The area we were fishing over was not very large, and I knew proper positioning of the boat would be important. I decided to drop the marker buoy over the location. I would then have a good visual as to where the boat stopped in proximity to the actual location of the mark. It took a couple of tries, but, because of the visibility of the marker buoy, we soon were over the spot, and were able to “Fish On.”

Often, knowing the perfect will of God for our lives can bring the same challenges and frustrations. We believe we know what God wants, but because of the winds and the currents of life, anchoring in that perfect spot in order to fulfill God’s purpose for us is difficult. This can be true in finding the right spouse, the right school, the right job, or the right ministry within the Kingdom of God. Allow the Holy Spirit to be a marker buoy that God can drop over the exact place where He wants you. It may take a time or two, or three or four, but anchoring in the exact location God wants you to be in will bring the kind of blessings and rewards you are seeking in your life.

Don’t be discouraged when you have to pull the anchor up and try again. God is patient, and willing to help us find that perfect anchoring spot.

Hebrews 6:19, “We have this hope as an anchor for the soul, firm and secure. It enters the inner sanctuary behind the curtain.”

Always Carry Plenty of Rope

Because the wind and current were moving strongly, I knew we would need to deploy extra anchor rode (rope) to make sure the anchor held firmly. The 150' I normally used would not be sufficient, so I got out the bucket with the 250' length. It would take a minute to exchange the rode, but the time would make anchoring in the deep water and strong current easier. Most mariners say you need a ratio of 7 to 1, or seven feet of anchor rode for each foot of depth. That figure can be as much as 10 to 1 in rough seas. It also helps if you can have several feet of chain between the anchor and the end of the rode; the extra weight of the chain making it easier to keep the anchor at the proper angle for a firm grip.

As you and I grow in the Lord, every trial or difficulty we overcome by the Holy Spirit is like adding extra feet to the anchor line of our faith. It's not that we are getting further away from the Lord. The extra length to which our faith has been challenged just provides us with more holding power, as the enemy continues to buffet us with the winds and adversities of life.

When God allows you and me to face that problem or difficulty, He may only be preparing us with some extra rope, so that the real trail the enemy has ahead for us will not pull our anchor of faith loose. That kind of spiritual strength and holding power in the storm does not come without a cost. Be willing to allow God to add the extra rope to your anchor.

Job 27:6, "My righteousness I hold fast, and will not let it go."

When the Skyline Disappears

It had been a great day on the water, and the fish had definitely been in an agreeable mood. The ice chest was full, and it would take some time to take care of the ones we were allowed to clean before getting back to the dock. Gene would be driving the boat, so I went over what he needed to do. Because there was a haze in the air, we could not clearly see the skyline of the buildings in Clearwater, therefore, he would have to run with the GPS. I put the boat on course and told him to stay on the indicated heading, moving left if he needed to decrease his bearing, or right if he needed to increase it. The skyline would come into view sooner or later, but, for now, we would have to depend on the GPS.

Many of us have been in situations in our lives where the spiritual skyline we had always counted on to navigate us is hidden by whatever we are facing. The pressure of the job can become so difficult that it is hard to see the sky-line of Christ out in front of you. Your relationship with your spouse may reach a critical point, and the pain become so severe that you just cannot seem to focus on God's love.

Even when you and I cannot clearly see our way, as we are surrounded by the problems and difficulties of life, God's Word is still the compass that never fails. The face of Jesus, and the skyline of your eternal hope, may not be visible right now, but His Word is still a sure compass to guide you.

Psalms 119:93, "I will never forget Your precepts, for by them You have preserved my life."

At Least, Teach What You Know

A friend from several years ago called to ask me for a favor. He had a friend from up north, who now lived close by, that wanted to learn about the coastal waters in our area. He needed to know where the shallow areas were, how to read the channel markers, and where he might find some scenic places he and his wife could go. He would be renting a boat, but, before he ventured out into the unknown, he was hoping someone would show him around. I was grateful for the opportunity to get out on the boat, and, also, for a chance to help someone who wanted to enjoy the beauty of our coastline.

As we live for the Lord, similar opportunities might present themselves to us. New believers, who do not know anything about their new walk and relationship with Christ, will need someone to take the time and opportunity to teach them what they need to know to walk in faithfulness. This is our chance to demonstrate what God has been faithful to teach us. Sometimes, our learning has been through the school of hard knocks, but, with our help, maybe they will not have to learn the same way.

I have lived and boated in this area for many years. I will not be able to teach this man all I know in a couple of hours, but, I will, hopefully, be able to show him enough that he will not find himself in a bad situation. Our spiritual guidance can help a new believer find real joy in serving the Lord, and how to avoid some of the pitfalls that we have experienced.

2 Timothy 2:24, “And the Lord’s servant must not be quarrelsome, but must be kind to everyone, able to teach, not resentful.”

Getting Too Close Will Cost You

The weight on the line, as I reeled it in, seemed to indicate that the fish would be a nice one. As the end of the line came into sight, it looked like I had a fish on each of the two hooks, but something looked a little funny. I finally realized that there were three fish on the two hooks. After getting caught by one of the hooks, the fish was struggling to free itself, while another fish was trying to get the bait out of its mouth. The second fish apparently got entangled in the line, and the pressure from the first fish kept the line tightly wrapped around him.

The enemy doesn't really care how he ensnares our lives, just so we are trapped by his deceptions and unable to break free. We may not think there is any real danger in the decisions we are making, but if we fail to recognize the danger present around us, we can easily become ensnared in something that will hold us captive and rob us of the freedom Christ purchased for each of us.

The second fish had not actually bitten the bait on the hook that day, but his close proximity to the caught fish left him vulnerable to the line that ensnared him. Don't find yourself trapped in a situation from which you cannot break free, just because you failed to see the danger that existed. Allow the Holy Spirit to speak to your heart, and prevent you from making what could be a very costly decision. You may not grab the hook, but, if you stay too close, you could still find yourself entangled in the line.

1 Corinthians 10:12, "If you think you are standing firm, be careful that you don't fall!"

Stay Aware of Changes

I watched the weather all week, but still was not sure about what to do for the planned trip the next day with my former youth pastor, now pastoring a great church in Deltona. He would be leaving his house at 6 A.M. to drive over, so I decided to wake up early, check the weather, and then make the decision. When I awoke the next morning, I was glad to see the winds had subsided enough that we would be able to make the trip.

Often as we seek to do something for the Lord, the opposition seems to confront us, even though it is our desire to do what God is asking. Of course the enemy will try to tell us that the opposition is because we are about to move out of the will of God, and that we are making a wrong decision. That is when we face some of our toughest choices. Do we move forward and believe the voice we hear is God calling us in this direction, or do we look at the opposition coming from so many directions and believe the voice of the enemy. God may allow opposition to help you see you are going in the wrong direction, but most often He will simply speak to you in the voice of the Holy Spirit. Opposition is most often a deception of the enemy to sidetrack us, or turn us away from what God is calling us to do. Stay focused on God and listen intently as you move forward. Don't change course just because the way looks difficult; listen to the voice of God.

Psalms 32:8, "I will instruct you and teach you in the way you should go; I will counsel you with my loving eye on you."

Preconceptions Can be Wrong

I had decided to place the 18' Bass Tracker up for sale, as I was not using it as much as I thought I would. After a good wash job and some wax, I took the pictures I would be posting and created the ad. As I was looking over the pictures, I commented to my wife about how nice it looked, the gloss on the gel coat was like new. I received a text right away from someone who made a ridiculously low offer for the boat without even seeing it. I told him I would not sell it that cheap, and that he needed to see the boat to know how nice it looked.

How many times do we tend to make quick decisions on things in our lives without really having all of the information? We criticize a ministry, question someone's motives, or even form a dislike of someone before we know all the facts. We even form opinions about people we have never met based on what someone else tells us, never giving that individual an opportunity. Let me challenge you not to make a decision before knowing and understanding all the facts. God may want to move you in a direction, and the enemy is opposing that move. When the men came to look at the boat, they admitted that it was worth what I was asking, and said they were glad they had taken the time to see it for themselves.

Don't miss what God has planned for you, because of a preconceived idea that probably came from the enemy. It could be an opportunity to meet a new friend God may be putting in your path.

Proverbs 21:5, "The plans of the diligent lead to profit, as surely as haste leads to poverty."

Some Things Are Out of Season

I knew the fish was a good size, because of the weight I felt and the fight it was putting up. I was excited to see what I had caught in the 60' of water where we were fishing. My excitement turned to disappointment, as the red snapper came into view. Although it is a prized fish, there is a season for them, and we were not in that time slot. I carefully removed the hook, and put it back into the water. I would have to wait for another day when the fish would be in season.

We face many things in our lives which seem to have seasons attached to them as well. If we are not careful, we can become disappointed, and even angry, because what we want now may not be in season for us, as far as God is concerned. The desire to get married may not be in season for us right now. The new job that will provide a great income for us is seemingly not in season, as well as many other things we want to have or do.

I may not agree with the regulations of the FWC, but I have agreed to abide by the regulations they have in place. The same is true in my spiritual life. I may not always agree with the Lord, but I have made a commitment to follow His will for my life, even when it is difficult. I knew there would be another day for the red snapper, and there will come another day for those things you are seeking as well.

Romans 8:28, "And we know that in all things God works for the good of those who love him, who have been called according to His purpose."

Lures Have a Hook and Barb

When a fisherman speaks of terminal tackle, he usually is talking about the hook at the end of the line. No matter what the quality of the rod and reel, the line, or even the expertise of the angler, unless the hook does its job well, you have little chance of landing the fish. A hook has two primary components. The first is the point of the hook. This needs to be sharp to penetrate the flesh of the fish when the hook set is made. The second is the barb. The barb Is the part that must prevent the hook from becoming dislodged during the fish's struggle.

The enemy of our soul is well acquainted with the terminal tackle he uses in his deceptions against us. He is always working to keep the hook of temptation extremely sharp, so that it can easily penetrate the life that gets too close. He also keenly knows how to keep the line tight, so the barb of lies and deception will not allow the hook to be easily dislodged.

Too many believers have discovered these truths by playing around with things that have sharp hooks with barbs. All may seem innocent at first, but the enemy is patently waiting to firmly set the hook in our lives. This part of the fishing gear is not called "Terminal Tackle" for no reason. The hook has only one purpose, and the lies the enemy feeds us have only one purpose. By the time you feel the sharp point of the hook, it may be too late to avoid the barb that quickly follows.

John 10:10, "The thief comes only to steal, kill, and destroy; I have come that they may have life, and have it to the full."

You Need Oil in the Trim Unit

The motor on the power trim and tilt unit of the boat's out-drive unit seemed to be working fine, but the out-drive was not coming up as it should. I checked all of the connections, and could not find any leaks or broken lines. I checked the owner's manual I'd received from the previous owner to see if I could find any clues as to what was wrong. It suggested I check the level of the hydraulic oil in the reservoir. I found the plug and when I removed it, I could not see any oil showing. I began adding the oil until it filled the reservoir, and began oozing out. I replaced the plug, and found the out-drive quickly responded to the controls.

Have you ever noticed that sometimes the motor of your spiritual life appears to be running well, but there is little real growth or accomplishment being made in your life. As the boat had a manual, our spiritual lives also have a manual that can help us discover what we need. God is faithful to help us diagnose the problem, and show us how to add the oil of the Spirit to the dry reservoir of our hearts. Don't just keep questioning why your spiritual life seems to be going nowhere. Go to the Word of God, and ask Him to search your heart... then make the necessary changes in your life. To remain content where you are is a dangerous situation.

Just as adding the hydraulic fluid to the trim reservoir solved my problem with the trim unit, a fresh supply of the Holy Spirit can do wonders for your spiritual life.

Ephesians 5:18, "Do not get drunk on wine, which leads to debauchery. Instead, be filled with the Spirit."

Don't Allow Trash in the Boat

The new subdivision, in which we live, had given me permission to park my boat in the back yard. I knew it would take a couple of weeks to move the aluminum shelter from where it had been to the house. That would mean the boat would be setting under the large oak tree, susceptible to the falling leaves and oak blooms. I have seen boats left open to that kind of situation, and I didn't want to face the cleanup. It would require purchasing a couple of tarps. By placing the protective covers over the boat, it would remain clean and ready for use until I moved the shelter.

Many times, we do not see the need to be constantly aware of what is going on around us in life. We forget we have an enemy, and he is watching for the opportunity to dump debris that can stain, corrode, or just dirty up our testimonies for Christ. It is too easy to believe that a few leaves or oak blooms will not make a difference. We fail to recognize that he will keep dumping into our lives, until we place the protective cover of the Holy Spirit over our hearts.

Yes, I could vacuum the boat occasionally, and even clean out the stains, but would it be ready when I wanted to use it? The same is true of our testimony for Christ. When we allow the enemy to dump in the debris of this world, it will not only dirty up our lives, but, many times, we are not ready to share our testimony because of it.

Job 17:9, "Nevertheless, the righteous will hold to their ways, and those with clean hands will grow stronger."

Is the Shelter Still Good?

The aluminum shelter that I used to park my boat under started out being a covering for an RV owned by a friend. I had dismantled it, and put it up at my house in Keystone. It served well there for several years. When we moved, I dismantled it again, and put it up at our new home. Now we were moving again, and I would, once again, dismantle the shelter and move it with me.

Sadly, there are few things in life which seem to have the resilience to continue to be useful, especially when time passes and circumstances change. Thank God, our lives in Christ can stand not only the test of time, but also stand the test of changing circumstances...even when circumstances come because we made choices that we knew would be harmful. Just like my aluminum shelter, our relationship with God can resist the storms of life that come, even when the paint may not be as bright and shiny as it once was. The foundation of God's promises that our relationship is based on will see us through.

Will this be the last time I move the shelter? I don't know. Is today the last time my relationship with God will be tested? I doubt it. What I do know is that as long as I continue to follow the voice of God, the relationship I have with Him will continue to serve me well.

Don't let the enemy cause you to fear just because your relationship with God has hit a bump or two. God is big enough to handle whatever the enemy throws at you.

1Corinthians 1:9, "God is faithful, who has called you into fellowship with his Son, Jesus Christ our Lord."

Don't Get Foul Hooked

As I sharply set the hook, I knew I had connected with the fish. The difficulty I was having reeling it in made me believe it was probably a good-sized fish. As it came within view, I realized it was just a regular-sized grunt that had become foul hooked. When you foul hook a fish, the hook gets caught in the fish in another place other than in its mouth. The fish you have foul hooked may not have even been after the bait, just in the wrong place at the wrong time when you set the hook hard.

You and I both know Christians who have been "foul hooked" by the enemy...maybe even ourselves. We all make poor decisions, being in the wrong place at the wrong time. It may have brought consequences to our lives that we never expected. Being with people who do not share our Christian convictions, dating someone who does not know the Lord, or watching something on the internet that we should not be watching all can place us in a position to be foul-hooked by the enemy. The outcome was not what we expected, but the consequences can be just as tragic.

The fish I foul hooked that day tasted just as good as if he had eaten the bait. No, I did not have compassion, and let him go because he was in the wrong place at the wrong time...neither will the enemy have any compassion on us. We cannot always avoid being in a bad situation, but we can be sensitive to the Holy Spirit, listen to His prompting, and not place ourselves in a position to be "foul hooked."

Haggai 1:7, "This is what the Lord Almighty says: 'Give careful thought to your ways.'"

It’s Different in the Dark

With no moon out, it was very dark when I pointed the boat southwest, and headed for our first mark. Both my grandsons were in front of the center console enjoying the ride. Suddenly, Kevin turned, and in a frantic voice said, “Turn around, Granddaddy, I think I saw a body in the water.” I turned the boat around quickly, and made my way toward where he was pointing. What I saw brought real concern, until we got close enough to see it was only the lifeless form of a large sea turtle, floating upside down. I remarked how glad I was it was not a body, first for the obvious reason of someone being dead, and, secondly, because our entire day may have been caught up in getting the authorities out there.

Sometimes in life, we are confronted with things that appear to be something they are not. We live in a dark world, and the enemy loves to make us believe we see things that are not as they appear at all. Lives have been damaged, and reputations destroyed, because something is said about someone without having a clear picture of what was actually going on. Accusations can be made, all because of what someone thought they heard. Because they did not know the whole story, they were way off-base.

It was important for us to know what Kevin really saw. It is also important that we are sure of our “information,” before we draw a conclusion that could hurt others. Be sure you are not making a dead body out of a dead sea turtle. The consequences to someone could be tragic.

Proverbs 16:28, “A perverse person stirs up conflict, and a gossip separates close friends.”

Keep Them Close to the Boat

The day of fishing had been great, and we were getting ready to run back to the dock. I noticed one of the fellows pointing at something close to the boat. I turned to see a mother and a baby dolphin, swimming within twenty feet of the boat, apparently scoping us out. I reached into the bait bucket, picked up a bait fish, and tossed it out to the larger dolphin. She quickly turned and grabbed the fish, as it was sinking. I reached for another bait fish, and, again, tossed it toward the pair of dolphins, who were now coming even closer. I was really excited, and took the next bait fish in hand. I began to splash the water next to the boat, and, almost on signal, the larger dolphin moved even closer. There are people that God puts in our lives that we have an opportunity to touch for the Lord. Our lives, hopefully, have modeled that of Christ, and they are coming closer to scope us out. Now is the time to lose our timidity, and begin tossing out portions of God's grace and mercy to attract them closer. Many people in the world are looking for what you and I possess in Christ.

Just as the dolphins stayed close, as we shared our bait fish with them, people will stay close to us as we share the love of Christ. No, the dolphins never came and ate out of my hand, and we can never be sure the person we are sharing with will accept Christ. However, we must make our best effort.

John 12:32, "And I, when I am lifted up from the earth, will draw all people to Myself."

Fishing Can be Good Close In

We had been fishing almost eighteen miles from shore. The fishing had been good, but now it was time for the long run back in. As I am prone to do, I was keeping a close eye on the fish finder as we were heading back. I noticed what appeared to be structure, or rocks, on the bottom. I knew this might hold fish, so I made a sharp turn and idled back over the area. It was hard to believe we were only three miles or so from the inlet, but I told the men we would see if there was any fish there. To my delight, we were soon pulling in some rather nice sized fish.

How many times have we wanted to go on a missions trip, or spend some time on a distant field of ministry, but, seemingly, the door would not open. It is easy to become discouraged, and feel like there will never be an opportunity to share the Gospel with those who need Christ. The sad irony is that the mission field is really only a few steps from our front door. Our friends and neighbors are often just as much in need of Christ as those in a foreign land.

I will certainly continue to venture off shore to those numbers 18-20 miles out. I will also be well aware that, if the weather does not permit the long run, there are fish just outside the inlet that can be caught. When He commanded us to go and preach the Gospel, Christ must have known about those just outside the inlet.

Acts 1:8, "You will be my witnesses in Jerusalem, and in all Judea and Samaria, and to the ends of the earth."

How Do We Interpret It?

In places where there is boat launching, marinas where boats are docked, or even near homes on the water, there may be a sign requiring minimum speed or no wake. It is amazing to watch the way people choose to respond to these signs. These are actually laws, the breaking of which can bring a hefty fine. Some will idle the boat and create little or no wake as they move forward. Others may slow down, but the boat is often putting out a good-sized wake at that speed. Some will throttle back, but are still up on plane, going much faster than they should be.

We see the same kind of mentality when it comes to the laws of God found in His Word. Some believers take seriously what God requires, and they walk in complete obedience to the mandate of Scripture. Others want to fudge a little, and have even come up with some clever lines to try to prove that what they are doing is alright. In reality, a wake is following behind them. Of course, there are those who ride the crest of "grace" to the extent that the laws were not made for them...after all, we are under grace and not law. The problem comes as we recognize that we did not make the law, and it will not be us who determines how it is interpreted.

The wildlife officer does not care that you didn't know that a little wake was still a problem. God is not seeking those who self-interpret the Law, but those who seek to walk as close to God and His ordinances as possible.

Hebrews 8:10b, "I will put my laws into their mind, and write them in their hearts."

Don't Get Trapped by Low Tide

I eased the 14' fiberglass boat toward the small tidal creek. I knew the water was shallow, but because the tide was flowing in, I knew there would be enough water depth to get inside the creek. Once inside, I could see why people made the effort to ease back into this area. It was a perfect habitat for the red fish that I was looking for. Because the tide was coming in, it only took a small amount of effort from the trolling motor to keep me moving, allowing access to the prime fishing area. After a couple of hours, I noticed the tide was changing, and I had to work the trolling motor harder to keep the boat in the best position. I stayed an hour or so longer before moving back to the mouth of the creek, only to find the water was now so shallow, it would be difficult to get out.

Sometimes, the Holy Spirit can be giving us subtle hints that it is time to exit the area of ministry that we have been enjoying. However, we can be so caught up in the success, that we refuse to acknowledge His voice. He may have to allow some difficulties or problems to be a means of stirring our attention, so we will be obedient to His command.

I was fortunate that day, and got out of the creek before the tide was too low. Don't allow your unwillingness to listen to the Holy Spirit, and be robbed you of what God may be calling you to do next. Learn to recognize the tidal flow of God's call in your life.

Ecclesiastes 3:1, "There is a time for everything, and a season for every activity under the heavens."

Is the Boat Talking to You?

As I drove into our subdivision, my eye immediately caught sight of the 24' Proline center console parked in the driveway. It had not been there before, so I was interested in who the owner was. I stopped by later when a man was outside cleaning the boat, and introduced myself. Mark and his family had moved in a few months before from up north, but I had never stopped to meet them. Now, I was standing in his driveway discussing the boat and the possibility of going out in it, so he could learn how to fish in salt water.

We may not always recognize that God is using an activity we enjoy to open a door for us to meet someone, and take the time to talk with them about the Lord. Mark's new boat was used by God to get me to stop, and meet this new family in our neighborhood. It only took a couple of times being out with him, enjoying a day of fishing, for us to begin building a relationship that would allow me to share my love for Christ. Do we get so busy that we miss a door of opportunity that God is bringing to us in order to share the Gospel? It is often through a relationship we build that we have the best opportunity to share what God means in our lives.

It may not be a new boat that gets your attention, but is God trying to direct you to someone that needs you...and the Lord? Does He see an opportunity for you to share Christ, one you may not have taken advantage of before?

Colossians 4: 5, "Be wise in the way you act toward outsiders; make the most of every opportunity."

More Than What We Can See

The grouper bait had been lying on the bottom for some time, but I had not seen any movement in the rod tip, or detected any sound from the clicker indicating a bite. I picked up the rod to check the bait, and out of habit, began to reel the line in slowly, just in case there was anything there. What a surprise when the line suddenly became very tight, and I felt the pull of a fish on the other end. I reeled hard, and pulled on the rod to set the hook. When I got the 24" red grouper in, I remarked to the fellows on board how surprised I was that the fish was even there, as there had been no indication anything was even attracted to the bait.

Our walk with Christ can bring similar surprises. We can be doing all the right things, working in a way that God surely could use what we are doing. Yet, for all our efforts, we seem to see no indications that anything is happening. I did my part...I put the bait down for the fish. The rest was not up to me. The results of your efforts are not always up to you. Don't get discouraged. If you continue to do what God requires, continue to place the bait out there for those who are lost, God will not be oblivious to your faithfulness. Many times, the Holy Spirit is working subtly, and we may not see any evidence that He is there. Be faithful, and when He prompts you to check your bait, you may be overwhelmed with what you find that He has done.

1Corinthians 4:2, "Now it is required that those who have been given a trust must prove faithful."

Defensive Mechanism is Great

The large pelican settled softly into the water near our boat. One of the men on the boat caught a small fish, and instead of letting it go, he tossed it in the direction of the bird. The pelican quickly grabbed the hapless fish before it had an opportunity to escape to the depths. Four or five more small fish were caught, and met the same demise. One of the men had just reeled in a puffer fish, so he tossed it in the same direction. To our amazement, when the pelican tried to turn the fish in its mouth, so he could swallow it, it began to puff up. In just a few seconds, the small fish was larger than a softball, and the pelican found it impossible to swallow. He let the fish fall from its mouth, giving it an opportunity to live another day.

Some people in the church find themselves falling prey to the enemy, having their lives attacked by the insatiable appetite of the deceiver. You and I, as believers, have a secret weapon of protection...if we are willing to use it. When the enemy of our soul attempts to swallow us up, the might of the Holy Spirit, and the power in the Word of God, can begin to cause our strength and courage to radically increase. The enemy finds it impossible to swallow us or defeat us.

The puffer fish knows he cannot defeat the pelican without allowing his body to rapidly inflate. You and I must also recognize that we cannot defeat the enemy unless we are willing to allow the Holy Spirit to increase and expand His presence in our lives.

1John 4:4b, "The One who is in you is greater than the one who is in the world."

Unseen Problems Can Cost You

Mike was enjoying a day on the water with us. It had been several weeks since he had been fishing, so this was a real treat for him. He had brought his own rod and reel that he had used many times before. As he continued catching fish, he suddenly commented that something seemed to be wrong with the reel. As we checked it out, we found two of the screws that held the reel to the mounting bracket had apparently worked loose, and the reel was in danger of coming off the rod. The screws were on the inside of the reel where you could not see when they worked loose. To make a repair would require taking the reel apart, and refastening the screws in place.

How many times have we discovered that some area of our lives in Christ seems to be coming apart, and, after checking things out, we find something going on off our normal radar screen? We are usually careful about the obvious spiritual maintenance, but often do not pay enough attention to those areas which are less noticeable. We are careful about what we say and do, but often allow our minds to wander dangerously. We are careful about the friends we keep, but do not seem to notice that what we are reading or looking at is out of line. Those four small screws holding the reel to the bracket could not be seen from the outside of the reel, but, without them, the reel was in danger of falling off the rod.

Don't allow the "little foxes to spoil your reel."

Song of Solomon 2:15, "Catch for us the foxes, the little foxes that ruin the vineyards. They may be small, but they are not insignificant."

Defeat the Swells of Past Sins

I was optimistic for a great day of fishing. The seas were going to be only 1-2 feet, according to the weather report. As we moved out of the inlet, however, I knew the meteorologist had missed it. The swells were more like 2-3 feet, maybe an occasional 4-footer, left from high winds the day before. We pointed the boat southwest, which was in the direction the swells were running, so we were able to make it to our fishing spot without too much difficulty. Once we were anchored, the larger swells were not bad, and the fish were biting.

Sometimes, when a person turns their life over to Christ, they may be expecting the seas of life to subside, and their journey with Christ to be easy. Unfortunately, the choices and the effects of our decisions before knowing Christ can create swells that do not go away overnight. Our salvation does not always undo the pain of a divorce, the medical effects of drug use, or the financial difficulties we are facing. God's grace brings unconditional forgiveness, but we are often still required to face the swells created by our lives before Christ.

You do not have to fear the swells. They will begin to diminish; it will just take some time. You can trust the One who called you will always be with you, no matter how the swells of life challenge you. When your heart is securely anchored in Christ, you can still accomplish what He called you to do, in spite of the swells created by the enemy.

Hebrews 6:19, "This hope we have as an anchor of the soul, both sure and steadfast, which enters the Presence behind the veil." NKJV

Not Always Easy for Beginners

It has always amazed me that it is necessary to take a written test and a driving test before receiving a driver's license, but none of that is necessary to operate a boat. It is especially surprising now that many boats are able to reach speeds above 50 MPH. You can purchase your boat, drive over to the boat ramp, and be a boat operator. The challenge often begins with trailering the boat. It only compounds when you get to the boat ramp, and find that backing the trailer is far more difficult than anticipated. Many times, these new owners have little or no idea as to the rules of the water, or what those red and green marker buoys mean. A little required training could go a long way when people purchase their first boat.

That is just as true when a person becomes a new Christian. Often there is little real discipleship for the new believer, and they quickly discover that living for Christ has many obstacles. Many may not understand that there are life changes that are necessary to make, and how we face problems and difficulties need to be different. Too often new believers struggle in their new walk with God, just as boat owners struggle to gain the knowledge they need to really enjoy their new purchase.

If you know a new believer, take some time to walk with them; explain to them what it truly means to know Christ. It will allow them to find the real joy that God has intended for them to experience in their new life.

Matthew 28:19, "Therefore, go and make disciples of all nations, baptizing them in the name of the Father and of the Son and of the Holy Spirit."

Trim Tabs Can Bring a Balance

Because my boat is a deep vee, it has a tendency to lean one way or the other, depending on the distribution of the weight of the men and fishing equipment with me. To compensate for that, I have a pair of trim tabs on the back of the boat that I can adjust to bring the boat back to a level ride. Even when the men may be moving around, I can simply push a button and the boat returns to level.

There are also times, in our spiritual lives, when things may become a little unbalanced. The attacks of the enemy may bring discouragement, distractions, or even anger and frustration. That is when it is great to allow the presence of the Holy Spirit in your life to operate the spiritual "trim tabs," and bring your life back to a level ride. He can bring you a special verse that will quicken your spirit, or a close friend that will speak a word of encouragement to you. He is great at bringing a spiritual balance to your life, so that even when things around you seem to be constantly changing, putting undue weight and pressure on your life, He can level things out for you.

There was a time, before I installed the trim tabs, that I would have to get the fellows to move from one side to the other to bring the right balance. Now, I just push a button.

Don't try to fix everything in your life on your own, so it will be on a level keel...trust God, and allow the Holy Spirit to bring balance to your life in His own way.

John 16:13, "But when He, the Spirit of truth, comes, He will guide you into all the truth."

All May Not Be as it Seems

It was dark as I launched the boat. After parking, I returned to the dock, and, as I proceeded to get things ready, I noticed one of the rods had fallen from the rod rack under the T-top. When I went to put it back in the holder, I noticed another rod was missing, also. I quickly realized it was the rod and reel I loved and used most often. I took a glance around the floor of the boat, and concluded the rod must have fallen out of the boat as I was driving over. My first feeling was irritation, but, as I thought a minute, I knew I should be thankful nothing else had happened. After all, I could have lost several of the rods, I could have had an accident coming over, and the list could continue.

How many times do we allow the old nature to dictate how we react to difficult situations in our lives, instead of allowing the Holy Spirit to bring a Godly response to things that are meant to disappoint? The enemy is a master at creating problems for us, bringing us discouragement and despair. You and I still have the ability, in Christ, to decide how we will react or respond. Choose to be thankful, no matter what the circumstances are.

Amazingly, not five minutes later, as I was near the back of the boat, I saw my rod and reel lying across the transom, wedged in by the live well, safe and sound. Would it have been there if my attitude had remained irritated? I'm glad that is a mute question now.

1Thessolonians 5:18, "In everything give thanks for this is the will of God in Christ Jesus concerning you."

Don't Ignore Warning Signals

We were idling out the Clearwater channel in the quiet morning darkness, when I heard the beeping and saw the red warning light on the engine gage flashing, indicating the engine temperature was high. I quickly shut the engine down, and took a minute to see if I could find a problem. Seeing nothing, I switched the engine back on and watched to see if the indicator would come on again. To my relief, the engine temperature was normal. We must have picked up something on the water intake, causing the engine to become overheated. Stopping the boat allowed whatever it was to fall away, and the engine quickly cooled down. I was grateful for the indicator that warned me of the problem.

God has also built into your life, and mine, a warning indicator, known as the Holy Spirit. He is constantly analyzing our spiritual lives, and is quick to warn us of any pending danger. The problem comes when we fail to pay attention to the warning indicators used by the Holy Spirit to signal a problem. It may be a word from a close friend, a message from the pastor, or a scripture verse that jumps out at us during our devotional time. Failure to heed the warning signals can place our lives and relationship with Christ in serious danger. When the warning comes, take time to stop a minute, and see what the Holy Spirit might be saying to you. To continue on, disregarding the warning indicator, is a sure way to damage your spiritual life. To repair an overheated engine can be costly, but a damaged spiritual life can be disastrous to you and those around you.

2 Corinthians 13:5a, "Examine yourselves to see whether you are in the faith; test yourselves."

A Power Source Is Necessary

The engine had started fine and the depth finder was coming on, but only one of the GPS units was working. I pressed the power button several times...nothing was happening. It was still dark, so I figured I would just check under the console later when the sun came up. I was glad to have the second unit on board. We proceeded to our first fishing location, and I pretty much forgot about the failed GPS. About noon, I decided to check the unit out and to my surprise, and amusement, I realized I had never plugged the unit in to the power supply. A quick plug in, and the unit was up and running as it was designed to do.

How often our day starts, as that day did for me, with something just not booting up right in our lives. We can become frustrated early with things not going right, and, often, the irritation continues to grow as the day moves on. We can even become critical with those around us, and allow our witness for Christ to suffer, all because the day didn't start right. My word of advice...did you plug into the Power Supply as you began your day? Did you take the time to get with the One who can bring peace and joy to your heart, no matter what the day may challenge you with? Fortunately, for me, I had a second GPS to utilize. In the spiritual realm, there is no substitute for being plugged into the power and anointing of God's presence. He is the only GPS we have available, and if we are not plugged into Him, we will quickly lose our way.

Psalms 63:1a, "O God, thou art my God; early will I seek thee."

A Reminder Can Save You

I had made the normal preparations on the boat the night before for the fishing trip. As I approached the dock, where I would meet the other men, I suddenly remembered that I had not placed the plug in the boat. I was surprised by this, because it was always something I did the night before in preparation for taking the boat out. I placed the plug in the boat, and said a special thanks to the Lord for allowing me to remember. Later, as I was sharing it with one of the men, he remarked that he thought about asking me about the plug just before we launched the boat. He was afraid I would be offended by the reminder. I told him to never be afraid to ask, because it was very important.

In our spiritual lives, it is also important that people feel free to ask us, and even to challenge us, when they see something that concerns them. Are we open to these remarks and challenges, or do we become offended that they are intruding where we feel they are not needed? I am grateful that when we may not be as sensitive to the nudging of the Holy Spirit as we should be, He is willing to place someone in our path who can speak His wisdom to our hearts. Life can become so hectic, so demanding, that we forget, or overlook, important areas in our relationship with Christ. Allow the Holy Spirit to speak to you through others, and you will find you can save yourself some real problems.

James 1:19, "My dear brothers and sisters, take note of this: Everyone should be quick to listen, slow to speak, and slow to become angry."

Dodging the Tentacles

As I set the hook and began to reel in the line, I was puzzled by what I was feeling. There was weight, but I couldn't really feel any movement on the line. As the end of the line came into view in the clear water, I saw the round head and the tentacles of the octopus struggling to free itself from the hook. Just as its head cleared the water, it began to squirt water out in a defensive mechanism. The question now was, "How do I get this thing off my hook?" As the octopus struggled to free itself, I could see where the hook was lodged, so I carefully maneuvered the knife to cut it loose. Every time I got close to the octopus, one of the tentacles, with its suction cups, would grab me. As I would pull it loose, another tentacle grabbed my hand.

The temptations of the enemy work in the same way as the octopus. All he needs for us to do is to get close, just make a small decision of indiscretion, and the tentacles will latch on to us. The suction cups will get a hold on us, and we may not be able to free ourselves. Even when we try to get free from one tentacle, we quickly find there is another that is reaching to get a hold on your life and mine. What we thought was a harmless choice can quickly become a matter of life and death, spiritually, for us and those around us.

I was able to make a small cut and turn the octopus loose that day, but freeing ourselves from the tentacles of the enemy may require a lot more effort.

Proverbs 2:11, "Discretion will protect you; understanding will guard you."

Be Smarter Than the Frog

I was enjoying the beauty of the smooth Gulf water, when, out of the corner of my eye, some movement caught my attention. I heard the splash, and saw the two-inch tree frog that had leaped from the boat and into the Gulf water. It remained motionless a few seconds, and then began swimming about. I remarked to the men in the boat, "That was a big mistake on the frog's part, to leave the safety of the boat for the predator infested Gulf waters."

The story of the prodigal son in the New Testament is very similar to what I witnessed with the tree frog. We often see people leave the safety of a life serving God to launch out into unknown "predator infested" waters. I'm sure the frog may have felt that getting away from the three people in the boat was a good choice. What he did not know was that leap, toward what he thought was a better choice, would place him in imminent danger. Before you make the choice you are planning, be sure you have checked with the only One who knows what is ahead. Be sure you are not taking a step that will place your life, and possibly others, in grave circumstances.

Your marriage may not be what you were hoping for, but that conversation with a co-worker may place you in predator infested waters. The church you attend may not be what you want, but don't leap before asking God what He would have you do.

Thankfully, a few minutes later, I saw the frog climbing back onto the boat transom...back to safety.

Psalms 25:12, "Who, then, are those who fear the Lord? He will instruct them in the ways they should choose."

Too Many Rods Can Cost You

The bite was slow, and I told the fellows to bring in their lines so we could move. I started the engine, and pointed the boat toward the next fishing spot. As I throttled back, and started maneuvering the boat to drop the anchor, one of the men noticed I had left one of my lines out when we moved. I seldom fish with just one rod, which allows me a better opportunity to catch fish. However, it can also cause problems at times. In my rush to move to a new spot, I had forgotten to bring in the line on my grouper rod. I checked the rod, and found that all the line had been spooled off the reel and ultimately broke off. It would now require refilling the reel before I could use it again.

In our service for the Kingdom of God, we can get so excited about working for Him that we get more rods out than we can adequately take care of. It might not be a problem at first, but unless we set priorities, we can find that we give the enemy an open door to create trouble that should not have happened. We can even miss a prime opportunity that God has for us, because we have become distracted doing something God never called us to do.

I still use multiple rods when I fish, however, the consequences of that action will seldom be as critical as taking on more than God has called you to do.

Romans 12:2, "Do not conform to the pattern of this world, but be transformed by the renewing of your mind. Then you will be able to test and approve what God's will is - His good, pleasing, and perfect will."

Let the Holy Spirit Keep it Dry

Many boats today are designed with two holes in the transom to allow water that may get into the boat to drain out automatically when the boat is underway. These holes usually have what are called scuppers on the outside of the hull that allow the water to exit, but not allow the water from the outside to enter the hull of the boat. If the scuppers are not working properly, water can seep back into the boat when you are anchored, a situation that can create serious problems.

When you and I come to know Christ, the Holy Spirit acts like a boat's scuppers, He works to remove things from our lives that allow the enemy an opportunity to break down our testimony for Christ. He also guards against anything coming into our hearts from the world around us that can create serious problems in our relationship with the Lord. Difficulties come when we do not maintain complete and utter submission to the will of the Holy Spirit in our lives. Disobedience handcuffs the Holy Spirit and what He was destined to do. Have you noticed influences of the world creeping back into your heart and attitude? Check the scuppers...they may not be working properly. Perhaps you are not submitting your will and choices to the Holy Spirit.

A little water in the boat can be easily removed by turning on the bilge; not so with areas in our lives being influenced by the world. That requires serious repentance, and close obedience to the Holy Spirit.

Psalms 139:23-24, "Search me, God, and know my heart; test me and know my anxious thoughts. See if there is any offensive way in me, and lead me in the way everlasting."

Know Your Defensive Weapons

If you have ever fished in salt water, one of the first things you learn is that many of the fish species have a strong defense mechanism. They may have sharp spines on their body, sharp gill plates that are like razor blades, or they may be able to inflate their body and swell to a point larger than the enemy that is trying to eat it can swallow. For some it is blazing fast speed; for others, it may be a toxin they can discharge when they are attacked. All of these are so they can defend themselves from predators which are constantly trying to capture and eat them. Using these defensive weapons effectively allows the fish a fighting chance against the constant attack of predators.

When you and I surrender our hearts to Christ, we are given an array of defensive weapons to protect us and keep us safe in our walk with the Lord. However, these weapons are of little use unless we learn how to use them against the enemy of our souls. The sword of the Spirit was never designed to be hung over a mantle in our spiritual lives, but was to be carried in such a way that it could be used at a moment's notice. The shield of faith provides little protection if left hanging on the wall.

The sooner a fish learns to effectively use its defensive weapon, the better chance he has to live through an attack from a predator. That should be enough said!

Ephesians 6:14-15, "Stand firm then, with the belt of truth buckled around your waist, with the breastplate of righteousness in place, and with your feet fitted with the readiness that comes from the gospel of peace."

Know What Attracts the Fish

As we were moving across the water to our fishing spot, I kept glancing at the depth finder. I have found good fishing spots by noticing something unusual about the bottom. It may be a sudden change in depth, a signature denoting a hard bottom, or even something sticking up that catches my attention. I have found that these things, attract fish. It may be an enticement because it provides hiding places for small bait fish, or it may be structure that is large enough to provide ambush points for large predator fish. Whatever it is, when I discover these locations, I will usually find fish, as well.

Our churches, and our lives, should also attract people, like these places lure fish. A church that is growing and adding to the Kingdom is a church that has found a way to attract people. When we know what people are looking for, providing those things will make us more appealing.

This is true in our individual lives. Our attitudes must be supportive, helpful, compassionate, and sensitive. If our church is meeting needs, encouraging hearts, and discipling believers, we will attract people. Everywhere that Jesus went, He was drawing people to Himself. If we, as God's Church, are not bringing people in, we need to meet the needs of those around us.

Artificial reefs are created by supplying the needs of the fish, thus attracting them. We are not Christ, but we have His Spirit in us.

John 12:32, "And I, when I am lifted up from the earth, will draw all people to Myself."

The Reason for Those Lights

It was still dark, as we left the dock for our fishing trip. Because of the darkness, we needed to turn on the front red and green lights, and the rear white light. These are the boat's navigation lights, designed so that other boats can see you and know what direction you are going in more than to actually provide light so you can see. These are not optional equipment, but a requirement for safety when boating at night. Sometimes, another boat being able to see, and accurately know what direction you are moving in, is critical when they may not actually be able to see your boat.

Navigational lights are also important in our spiritual lives. We may know where we are going and what we are planning on doing, but it is also important that we give clear signals to those who are also working for the Kingdom of God near us. We have all seen situations that caused hurt and damage because there was no clear signal as to what was going on, or what direction a person or ministry was taking. We must never see our lives or ministry as the only boat in the water. God has called us to work close to one another, and clear navigational lights will allow us to operate safely. The world around us is dark, and spiritual visibility is not always good, but we can make sure our direction and purpose for God is not in doubt.

Just assuming people know what you are doing is not enough; we need clear spiritual navigation lights.

Psalms 43:3, "Send me your light and your faithful care, let them lead me; let them bring me to your holy mountain, to the place where you dwell."

Give Everyone Their Own Space

The weather was perfect, and we were looking forward to idling up the Weeki Wachee River. The river was narrow, and there were many kayakers on the river, as well. I had to really keep my eye on things, as we were in a 24' boat, and things were always crowded. It was also important to watch the depth of the river, and realize that just because kayakers could navigate in areas, there might not be enough depth for my large boat. All of us on the river could enjoy the beauty of the scenery, but each of us had to recognize our limitations and the limitations of those around us.

Living for God also requires each of us to recognize limitations, not only in our lives, but in the lives of those traveling with us. Perhaps, you have been a part of God's Kingdom for many years, therefore you are required to travel in deeper water than those who have only been saved a short time. We need to remember that because we have been saved longer, people are often looking to us and our lives to have a greater impact than those who have only known the Lord a short time. Each of us can enjoy the beauty and the joy of traveling through life as part of the Kingdom of God, as long as we don't lose sight of those around us who are also traveling this river. Because I was careful and respectful of the kayaks, even though they were smaller, we all had a great day on the river. Don't be the reason someone missed the joy and beauty in serving God.

Amos 3:3, "Do two people walk hand in hand if they aren't going to the same place?"

Don't Underestimate the Fish

The clicker on the large reel went off, and Mark and I looked at each other, knowing it was a big fish. He pulled the rod from the holder, and set the hook on the fish. The fish made a hard run around the front of the boat and under the anchor rope. I was afraid it would tangle in the anchor rope, so I rushed to the front of the boat. I leaned out, and told Mark to hand me the rod, so I could pass it under the anchor line and avert the danger. I felt certain the large fish was just a shark, but to my surprise, and Mark's great delight, a few minutes later, a large 28" Gag Grouper was alongside the boat.

How many times have we watched as God has touched the life of someone, and in our mind we were grateful that they came to know the Lord, but in reality we had no idea the kind of plan God had for their life. Who would have thought the rag tag group that Jesus had chosen as His apostles could turn the world on its heels? Who would have believed that the man persecuting the Church would be used to touch kings with the Gospel?

I'm glad we made every effort to hang on to the fish that day, and not make only a half-hearted effort because I thought it was "just" a shark. Remember, the life God is using you to touch is more than just another soul in the Kingdom...they could easily be another Paul or Peter.

Acts 9:15, "But the Lord said to Ananias, 'Go! This man is my chosen instrument to proclaim my name to the Gentiles and their kings and to the people of Israel.'"

Take Care of the Little One

Chris wanted to spend some dad-time with his 10 year old son, Nathan, so he asked if we could take an offshore fishing trip. All I need is an excuse to go fishing...especially to help a young person come to love fishing, too. From the time Nathan came aboard the boat, there was one question after another. When we arrived at our first fishing spot, it was necessary to explain how to work the reel and set the hook. It only took a few minutes, and Nathan had his very first fish coming in. The excitement as he fought the fish, and then held it for pictures was really special. There were times when he did not understand everything and a lot more questions had to be answered, but helping him learn to love fishing was worth all the inconveniences.

How true it is, also, when we are working with a newborn child of God. There are so many questions, and it seems we are always trying to explain something they don't know or understand. Just as watching Nathan catch that first fish was the highlight of the day, watching a new Christian come to a place of really knowing and loving God is a special privilege.

I really hope that the first experience that Nathan had will set the tone for his love for fishing in the future. We also can play a big role in how new Christians view their walk and relationship with Christ. A little patience and a lot of love will do the trick.

Luke 17:2, "It would be better for them to be thrown into the sea with a millstone tied around their neck than to cause one of these little ones to stumble."

Not All Can Pull the Anchor

Many times, when I am fishing, I have individuals with me who are in their "mature" years. Because of their age, it is often difficult for them to pull the anchor in for me when we are changing locations. For that reason, I often ask one of my grandsons to go along on the fishing trip. Their young, strong arms and backs can usually make short work of pulling in the anchor, especially if we move often during the day. They know when I ask them to go that their responsibility on the trip will be that of "anchor man."

In the work of the Kingdom of God, we need to also understand that not everyone has the same talents and skills, nor do they all possess the same spiritual strength and faith. What may seem to be an overwhelming obstacle for one may be only a minor bump in the road for another. The Holy Spirit is the only one who really knows the strength and ability possessed by a child of God. In the Kingdom, we should be careful that we are not quick to criticize the way people handle, or mishandle, the struggles they face. The Holy Spirit is the one working to achieve His goals in their lives, and our part is to help and encourage them, as they walk through the difficulties and problems they must face.

The fellows with me on the boat are always glad when I tell them Kevin or Brandon is going to be with us, and take care of the anchor pulling for the day. Of course, Kevin and Brandon get to fish as their reward for pulling the anchor.

Romans 15:1, "We who are strong ought to bear with the failings of the weak and not to please ourselves."

Is the Anchor Firmly Attached?

A few years ago, I was fishing with some friends, and my oldest grandson, Kevin. Because he was young and strong, Kevin was voted to be the anchorman. As we came to our next location, I told him to drop the anchor and I would back the boat up to the desired spot. Kevin threw the anchor out as usual, and I watched, as if in slow motion, as the end of the anchor rope slipped through his hands and disappeared overboard. The look of disbelief on his face was priceless. The anchor was on the bottom, and the other end of the rope was not attached to the boat.

This can be true in our lives. We can confess that Jesus is the anchor, but if that anchor is not firmly attached, it is about as useless as the anchor was that day on the boat. We keep that anchor tied to our lives by walking closely with the Lord, and living in obedience to the Word of God. The enemy loves to deceive us, as to whether or not the anchor is firmly attached. He knows that the consequence of not having the anchor firmly attached is that your life will continue to drift off the mark. When the trials of life come, don't watch in dismay as the anchor line of your life slips overboard. Tie a solid knot by walking in obedience to the Word of God. Don't make an assumption that it is secure, only to find out too late when it slips overboard. Keep the boat firmly affixed to the Anchor of your life.

James 1:22, "Do not merely listen to the word, and so deceive yourselves. Do what it says."

Let God Determine Your Place

As the fellows arrived who would be fishing with me on this trip, each of them had certain things they had brought with them. There were tackle boxes, and ice chests with lunch and something to drink. I took the things they handed me, and carefully placed them in compartments around the boat to keep from having any more things than necessary on the deck. Running offshore, especially if it is a little choppy, can cause things to get tossed around. Besides, it is difficult to fish if you cannot move around easily on the boat. Because it was my boat and I was the captain, and the one responsible for everyone's safety and comfort, they were willing to allow me to make the necessary decisions for stowing the gear.

When we become a part of the Kingdom of God, we also have to learn to allow the Holy Spirit to take what we bring with us, and place it where He deems best for our welfare and that of others in the Kingdom of God. The church where we will serve, the job where we will be a witness for Christ, even the friends He wants us to reach out to are all to be determined by the Holy Spirit.

Just as the fellows were willing to allow me to make those decisions on the boat, we must be willing to allow Him to make those decisions in our lives and the Church. Just as I made decisions that would benefit those fishing with me, God makes His decisions to benefit us and His Kingdom.

1 Corinthians 12:18, "But in fact God has placed the parts in the body, every one of them, just as He wanted them to be."

More Than Just a Pretty Wrap

I had seen the new wraps that were available for boats, and thought one would be a great way to dress up the boat I have owned for 20 years. Over that period of time, the salt water, the salt air, and the bumps and scrapes from contact with the docks have taken a toll on the luster and sheen the boat once had. I spoke to the man at the wrap store about what it would cost, and also about the durability of the wrap material. I was disappointed to find that the wrap would not be able to take much hard contact with the docks without damage. It would basically provide a pretty exterior, but little protection for the boats finish.

The relationship many have with Christ is much like the wrap I was looking at. It may dress up the outside, somewhat, but does little to actually protect their inner spiritual life. As long as they don't hit any rough docks, or difficulties that would mar the finish, it will continue to shine and look good. Our lives are seldom without problems and pressures. Life can become a series of bumps and scrapes that are always trying to mar our testimony for Christ. Real durability in our spiritual lives requires more than just "a wrap" in our relationship with God. There must be genuine depth and commitment in our walk and relationship with Christ if we are to continue to keep a beautiful exterior finish in our spiritual life.

I did not put a wrap on the boat, and I pray my spiritual life is more than just a wrap, also.

Ephesians 5:8, "For you were once darkness, but now you are light in the Lord. Live as children of light."

What Size Cleat is Needed?

Whether parked at the dock, or pulling away from the dock, it is often necessary to attach or detach the rope from the cleat on the boat. The cleat is a device attached to the boat that allows you to secure something to the boat with a rope, or to secure the boat to a dock or something with a rope. The size of the boat, or what you need to secure to it, will determine the size the cleat needs to be. It matters little how strong the rope is, or how secure the other end of the rope is fastened, if the cleat on the boat is not up to the task. The same is true if it is not securely fastened to the boat.

Faith operates the same way in our spiritual lives. Faith is what is used to connect us to the things of God, but also what the Spirit will use to connect our lives to Him. Jesus is that immoveable force and foundation that we need to which we secure our faith. However, like the cleat that may not be up to the task we require of it, our faith may also lack the strength to hold us securely to Christ. It's foolish to place a cleat designed for a kayak on a large cabin cruiser, and expect it to serve its purpose. Make sure the faith in Christ that is the cleat in your life is sufficient to withstand what the enemy throws your way. Just as the boat can drift from the dock if not secure, so can our love for Christ.

2 Thessalonians 2:15, "So then, brothers and sisters, stand firm and hold fast to the teachings we passed on to you, whether by word of mouth or by letter."

There is Value in the Church

Most boats today, designed specifically to be fishing boats, have a center console and T-top. This configuration is especially beneficial because the center console and T-top are placed in the boat in such a way that when you are fighting a fish, you can walk completely around the boat's interior without interference. The center console provides storage, a place for the steering wheel and controls of the boat, even shelter from the wind. The T-top is designed to provide shade on hot days, and also to hold other equipment and life jackets as needed.

The Church was also specifically designed to meet the needs of spiritual fishermen. It provides a place for steering and control, as well as a place for storage and protection from the attacks of the enemy. The Church also allows a great deal of liberty to seek out and achieve the gifts and calling that God has placed on your life.

You can still fish out of a boat without a center console and T-top, but you forfeit so many of the benefits they were designed to provide for the avid fisherman. You can still do ministry outside of a local body of believers... "a church," but you will find yourself often exposed to many more of the enemy's attacks than are necessary. There will, also, not be the help and support God intended through the Church.

The center console and T-top does not make the boat perfect, but it is a tremendous help to the fisherman. The Church is not perfect either, but there really is no second choice that works as well in the Kingdom of God.

Matthew 16:18b, "On this rock I will build My Church, and the gates of Hades will not overcome it."

Need a Pair of "Son Glasses"?

The expression, "You've come a long way baby" could certainly be used to describe the use and development of sunglasses. This facial wear is no longer just a means of shading our eyes from the sun, or making us look "cool," but they have evolved to meet many different needs for people. I appreciate a good pair of polarized sunglasses to help remove the glare that often prevents me from seeing into the water clearly. It can give the fisherman a great advantage when sight fishing for many of the species that frequent the shallow waters. By filtering out the glare of the sun, you are able to see more clearly what may be hiding in the water.

The same is true when we learn to look through the eyes of Jesus, and allow Him to be our Son Glasses. The enemy, and the glare he brings from the worldly culture around us, can prevent us from seeing clearly what God wants us to see. By being a filter for our eyes, Jesus can eliminate the glare that can hinder our clear thoughts and decisions.

Clear vision helps us to be more effective for God's Kingdom, and better recognize the needs of those around us. One sunglass maker's slogan is, "See what's out there." Maybe the Church needs to encourage each of its followers to get a pair of "Son Glasses," and take a look at the world around them. Make sure you can "See what's out there," and you will find it easier to fulfill God's call on your life.

Luke 6:42a, "How can you say to your brother, 'Brother, let me take the speck out of your eye,' when you yourself fail to see the plank in your own eye?"

A Light Makes It Easier

The men that were going fishing with me were excited about the trip, but I could sense a little concern as it was still very dark when we pulled away from the dock. We idled into the channel, and I turned on the million candlepower spotlight to help us illuminate our path. I also directed their attention to the two GPS units on the dash of the boat. The display screen on the GPS not only showed our location and progress, but it also marked out the channel in a different color so there was no doubt about the path we needed to take.

As believers in Christ, how blessed we are to have the power and presence of the Holy Spirit in our lives to help illuminate the path ahead as we walk in Christ. His wisdom and guidance are wonderful tools to help us keep our hearts on the right path of life. The Word of God also acts as a great GPS, marking out where the spiritual channel of life runs. Even when we may have some questions and concerns about what to do, or which way to turn, if we will keep a close eye on His Word, we never need to venture out of the channel that it marks out for us. The darkness around us can be somewhat scary at times, but God has provided us with powerful tools to help us navigate life. When the darkness seems to overwhelm all that is going on around you, allow your spotlight of the Spirit, and your GPS of Scripture to bring you peace as you navigate in the darkness.

Psalms 119:105, “By your words I can see where I’m going; they throw a beam of light on my dark path.”

Add Weight to the Gospel

There are many things in the sport of fishing that have literally revolutionized the way we fish. One of these is the lowly lead head jig. It has evolved from its early inception of simply being a weight attached to the eye of the hook, to literally having eyes that move. Some even have rattle chambers to attract the fish. Who would have dreamed that adding a lead weight to a hook could change the presentation and its effectiveness so much?

In reality, Jesus understood this concept more than 2000 years ago. He realized the message of the Gospel was indeed a hook that could catch people. He knew that when that hook had a head, even hands and feet, and especially a compassionate heart, it would become so much more effective in attracting people to its message. There are those who simply, by reading the Word of God on their own, will come to know Christ, but, by far, the majority of people who get hooked by the Gospel have had someone talk to them, show love and compassion to them, and be the heart and voice of Jesus Christ.

The lead head on the hook is not the hook that catches the fish, but it has become a powerful way to effectively present the bait. You and I can never reach a person on our own for Christ, but when our lives model the Gospel, we become the bait God uses to attract that person to God. How can God use you to make His plan more effective in a life?

Matthew 5:16, "In the same way, let your light shine before others, that they may see your good deeds and glorify your Father in heaven."

Are We on the Same Page?

Mike was excited that we had a day scheduled to go fishing offshore. The day before we were to leave, I asked if he had been offshore fishing before, intending to encourage him to take some Dramamine, in case he was susceptible to seasickness. He said he had been offshore often, so I didn't feel the need to say anything to him. He arrived at the dock on time, and soon the bow of the boat was pointed west and moving across the water. After about ten minutes, when we were a couple of miles offshore, he looked at me, and said, "Wow, I've never been this far off-shore before." I knew it was going to be an interesting day. Apparently Mike's definition of fishing "offshore" was very different than mine.

The same can be true when we talk to others about walking with Christ. What one person understands as righteousness and holiness can be very different from another person's point of view. What one person recognizes as the voice of God may be vastly different than another person's. There have been many problems and situations arise within the body of Christ because some Christians used the same terminology, but had a very different understanding of what was meant.

As Mike and I reached our first fishing spot, and I shut off the engine, I watch the color drain from his face. I knew it would be a long day. As believers in Christ, we need to be sure those we are communicating with about our faith are on the same page.

1Peter 3:8, "Finally, all of you, be like-minded, sympathetic, love one another, be compassionate and humble."

Need a Buffer in Your Life?

The propeller on a boat can often strike something in the water, or even the bottom in shallow areas. The force can easily be enough to damage the propeller to an extent that it would not be usable anymore. A safety factor built into the design of the propeller is a rubber hub that is pressed between the propeller and the hub spline. It can give somewhat when the propeller strikes a significant object. The rubber hub may not prevent all the damage, but it can often limit the damage significantly.

In our walk with Christ, our choices and decisions can place our lives, both natural or spiritual, in circumstances that could bring great damage. It was our decision, and the Holy Spirit may not prevent us from striking the object, but He can limit the damage. God will not allow the enemy to completely destroy us. Just as the rubber hub can mean the difference between not only damaging the prop, but also the motor it is attached to, the Holy Spirit can provide the protection necessary to keep us from complete spiritual destruction.

If you continue to strike objects with the propeller, eventually the rubber hub can be damaged. It will no longer allow the transfer of power between the engine shaft and the propeller. The same truth is found spiritually...to continue to make poor choices will set you up to lose the power of God working in your life. To continue to make poor choices, trusting in the Holy Spirit to bail you out, is little more than testing the Lord.

Matthew 4:7, “Jesus answered him, ‘It is also written: Do not put the Lord your God to the test.’”

Watch for the Kinks in Life

The fellows were on time, and soon we were idling out the Cotee River toward the bait traps I had set out the day before. We were looking forward to a great day, and we would have live bait. As we reached the marker where we could speed up, I pressed the throttle forward and the boat was soon on plane. After about three minutes, the engine just died, as if I had switched it off. We checked some things, then pumped up the gas ball again, and the engine restarted. The same thing happened two more times, and we decided it best to go back in so I could find out what the problem was. When I got the boat home, and removed the cowling, I noticed the gas line under the cowling was kinked, not allowing enough gas flow to keep the motor running at high speed.

The same is possible in our spiritual lives, when the flow of the Spirit is kinked, or interrupted, because of poor choices or decisions we are making. When we are too busy to spend time in His word or in prayer, or even in the house of God, the kink caused by these choices can prevent a sufficient flow of the Spirit into our lives to keep us strong and faithful to the Lord.

The motor was an easy fix, as I straightened the hose out. Making the right choices will fix the problems in our lives as well, and we will begin to sense a fresh flow of the Spirit.

Psalms 51:11-12, "Do not cast me from your presence, or take your Holy Spirit from me. Restore to me the joy of your salvation and grant me a willing spirit, to sustain me."

Sometimes it Takes a Knife

As we walked up to the garage sale, I noticed several different sized anchors lying on the ground. I asked the man at the sale how he came to have so many anchors, and especially of different sizes. He told me he was a scuba diver, and that he had found the anchors on his dives. If you have owned a boat, you know the sick feeling when you try to pull the anchor in and realize it is caught solid in the rocks. Often it is too deep to retrieve, and no amount of pulling with the boat will dislodge it. Sometimes the only option is to cut it loose.

Many who come to Christ often find that some old part of their flesh man is much like those anchors. They have made a commitment to Christ, and they are looking forward to beginning a new life. That old anchor is buried hard and fast, and they just can't seem to pull loose. Breaking free may require doing something drastic. It may require a step that is hard to make, but is the only solution. That addiction to pornography, drugs, alcohol, or smoking may have such a hold on your life that you cannot pull it loose; it must be cut off.

Refusing to cut an anchor loose requires you to be willing to remain where you are anchored. Refusing to get the kind of help you may need to defeat that addiction in your life dooms you to remain in bondage. Make the right choice for your life; cut it loose before it is too late.

Galatians 5:1, "It is for freedom that Christ has set us free. Stand firm, then, and do not let yourselves be burdened again by a yoke of slavery."

Unwritten Rule on the Water

Mark and I launched the boat, and began the slow idle to the mouth of the Cotee River to set out the bait traps for the next day's fishing trip. We spotted the 24' bow rider near the channel right away. Because the tide was out, I knew the boat was in a shallow area. I asked Mark if he thought they might need some help, but he didn't know for sure. As we got closer, I saw the anchor was down. Sure enough, they said they had motor trouble and the boat was aground. We maneuvered in close, and the man on the boat threw us a rope to tow him back to the marina. It took a couple of minutes to pull them free, but soon the boat was moving and we were headed toward the marina a few hundred yards away. The man wanted to pay me for the help, but I told him he didn't owe me anything, because I might need help one day myself.

In our journey for the Lord, we may sometimes come across those who have run into difficulties in life and just need a little help and understanding. Are we quick to ask what they might need, or do we just assume that all is well and continue on about our business? It is an unwritten rule on the water that you do not leave someone stranded, or in trouble, if you are able to help. That unwritten rule on the water is a written rule in Scripture when we see a brother or sister in trouble.

Matthew 25:40, "The King will reply, 'Truly I tell you, whatever you did for one of the least of these brothers and sisters of mine, you did for me.'"

Dirty Shoes Can Leave a Mark

I was amazed at all the different boats at the boat show that year. We were walking around, and looking at all the different shapes and sizes. As we prepared to climb aboard one of the new center consoles, I noticed the sign that asked that shoes be removed before coming aboard. They were trying to prevent the dirty shoes from leaving shoe prints on the floor of this beautiful and expensive boat.

I wonder if a sign like that might be a good idea in our spiritual lives. How often we allow someone, or something, to deposit into our hearts and minds "dirt" that leaves its unsightly mark on the beautiful and expensive life God has created in us. It may be a person, or some form of media that we have been listening to or watching. The marks are easier to get there than they are to remove. Words, ideas, and images planted in our hearts and minds can quickly take root and be extremely difficult to deal with. They seem to linger long after they are deposited. They can continue to create for us constant struggles...even years later. Some pictures or thoughts may be impossible to remove outside of the work of the Holy Spirit.

We should never post a "Do not enter" sign on our lives, as we need to be salt and light to the world. However, we can post a "Please remove your shoes" sign, and make sure the footprints of those who are walking around in the world are not left on our hearts and minds. It is up to us to keep the "boat" of our lives clean.

Proverbs 4:23, "Above all else, guard your heart, for everything you do flows from it."

A Weatherman Can be Wrong

Don and the three men from his church were on time and excited about the day of fishing. The weatherman, the day before, said the winds would be 5-10 knots and the seas two feet or less. As we were leaving the dock, we all noticed the winds seemed to be a little stronger than was predicted, but the excitement of the day of fishing was not dampened. As we moved out of the Clearwater inlet, I knew the weatherman had missed it...again. We were in steady 2-3 foot seas, and, before the day was over, we would be bouncing around in 3-4 foot chops.

The life we live in Christ can often be the same as that day of fishing. We can go into a relationship believing God has placed us there, and, suddenly, everything goes south and we are questioning God. We can accept a new job that promises to be everything we could want, and then a new manager steps in and we hate the thought of going to work each day. We make plans for an exciting vacation, only to begin to feel some discomfort and have the doctor tell us we need emergency surgery.

Life, just like the weather, does not always go as we have planned, or as someone has promised it will go. We may not always have a choice in what life, or the weather, throws us, but we do have a choice in how we will respond or react to it. Don't allow what life throws your way to dictate your response. Define who you are, and how you will face life's challenges by your attitude.

1Thessalonians 5:18 (MSG), "Thank God, no matter what happens. This is the way God wants you who belong to Christ Jesus to live."

Make Sure You're in Position

When I am fishing offshore, I often mark the location of the reef with a marker buoy. It is an orange flag, positioned on a float, tethered to a line and weight that is dropped over the exact location of the reef. I know that if the boat is not anchored in the correct position over the reef, I will have less chance of finding the fish I am looking for. The same is true in our spiritual lives. We sometimes miss what God wants to do, because we are out of position spiritually. If we want to receive the breakthrough and blessings that God has promised, we will need to be in the right place, at the right time, to receive that promise. The enemy is very adept at causing us to drift off position, making us lose patience with God and move too soon, or causing us to doubt and just give up hope. He doesn't care what we believe, or why we are out of position, as long as we are not in the right position for the spiritual breakthrough God has prepared for us. We will not just stumble upon spiritual breakthrough and blessings in our lives. God does not just fling out His blessings and breakthroughs in a haphazard manner. They are strategically placed and designed to build and develop our lives into the likeness and image of His Son Jesus Christ.

Spiritual breakthrough will only be possible as we determine to make the choices and decisions that will place us in the God-desired position to receive those breakthroughs.

2 John 1:8, "Watch out that you do not lose what we have worked for, but that you may be rewarded fully."

Helping Others Brings Reward

I was really looking forward to fishing with the youth pastors who would be joining me on this trip. I really enjoy taking people out who have never experienced this kind of offshore fishing. As we got set up on the first number, I placed my grouper line in the water, and let the lead take the live pinfish to the bottom. It only took a minute for the clicker to begin making that familiar noise that signaled a fish. I tightened the line and set the hook, immediately knowing this would be a good fish. I quickly handed the rod to the youth pastor standing next to me, and told him to fight the fish. As he took the rod and felt the strength of the fish, the look of excitement on his face was enough to tell the story.

When we are serving the Lord and not self, watching someone else get pats on the back, or the recognition for something we also had a part in, does not bring jealousy, but a great feeling of being a part of something much greater than we are. Much work for Christ has lost its effectiveness, because there was a struggle over who would get the credit or the recognition. We need to be constantly reminded that God is completely aware of every situation, and all that was involved in accomplishing His will. He will always give credit where credit is due. When we push in to get the acclaim, we have already received our reward. When we put others ahead of ourselves, then we have a reward that will last forever in heaven.

Matthew 6:4, "Let your giving be in secret. Then your Father, who sees what is done in secret, will reward you."

The Repair Work Can be Messy

The gel coat was cracking and breaking away from the inside of the fiberglass on my boat, so I decided to do some repair work. I got the angle grinder, placed the sanding pad on it, and started removing the gel coat that was loose. It took a few minutes, and when I turned the grinder off I noticed I was covered with gel coat dust, as was everything in the boat's interior. What I thought would be just a minor repair of the gel coat was now going to also be a major cleanup.

Often in our lives, when there are areas that need some attention and repair, we fail to see the full extent of what that repair will require. I knew that all the old loose gel coat needed to be removed, but I wasn't thinking about the mess. God knows that what we see as the necessary repair process may not be sufficient to do the job right. Some issues in our lives have deep roots in our past, and, sometimes, even in our family history.

Even as the dust continued to mount in the boat, I kept grinding until I knew that every area of loose gel coat was removed. God wants to do the same for us. The process to bring victory may not always be pretty and painless, but the results God will bring will be worth it. The boat is now ready for a brand new layer of gel coat in those areas that were cracking and breaking.

What does God have planned for your life when the repair work of the Spirit is complete?

Romans 6:6, "For we know that our old self was crucified with Him, so that the body ruled by sin might be done away with."

Don't Let Darkness Blind You

Casey, and his two friends, met me at the dock at six, as I had instructed them to do. It was still dark, and there was also a heavy fog that had settled in, making it even darker. We eased away from the dock, but the large spot light on the T-top was just not cutting through the fog well enough to spot the channel markers. Fortunately, the GPS I was using distinctly marks out the channel in a bright contrasting color. Even though we could not see where the channel ran by the markers, we were able to simply follow the GPS and stay on course.

Many times in life it can seem we are surrounded by darkness. To make matters even worse, we are struggling with confusion, sometimes because of those who are trying to give us advice. We want to stay in the will of God, but we just can't seem to see the next channel marker we need to stay on track. Fortunately, the Word of God distinctly lays out a path that we should follow as we make choices and decisions in life. Just like my GPS, we have to learn to understand what it is saying, and trust the information it is giving us. I had been out that same channel many times before. It would have been easy to just trust my instincts, but that would have certainly gotten me into trouble.

Don't find yourself stuck in shallow water; learn to study and follow God's GPS...the Bible. We made it out that day, and enjoyed a great time of fishing, thanks to the guidance of the GPS.

Psalms 119:59, "I have considered my ways, and have turned my steps to Your statutes."

Removing the Triggers in Life

If you have had the opportunity to fish offshore, you may have had the good fortune to catch a triggerfish. Besides being delicious to eat, the triggerfish has a unique quality. Just in front of its dorsal fin are two sharp and strong spikes. The first is usually about three times as long as the one just behind it. If you try to push the larger spike backward and down, you will find it can't be done. No matter how hard you push, the spike does not move. Those who have seen this before usually know why it's called a triggerfish. If you push the second spike, the "trigger," back first, the larger spike will follow with it, and also lay down on the fish. The smaller spike may not seem as important at first glance, but, without it, the larger spike will not lay down.

You and I are often raised in this world with "triggers." They are traits and issues that can seem to break down and destroy our ability to stand strong when the enemy brings temptations. Often, just when we think that we will be able to stand and defeat the enemy, he pushes our "trigger," and we seem to cave in. When we consider the "triggers" in our lives, we should never see them as small, or unimportant. Unless we are willing to allow the Holy Spirit to help us defeat these little "triggers," we will always struggle in our walk with Christ.

Ask the Lord to help you to defeat the "triggers" in your life, and learn to walk in the victory He has promised.

Song of Solomon 2:15, "Catch for us the foxes, the little foxes that ruin the vineyards, our vineyards that are in bloom."

Fog Hides the Channel Markers

As we eased away from the dock early that morning, the fog had settled in. The man driving the boat was commenting on how many times he had been out this channel, so he was not concerned. The boat we were following had disappeared into the fog, and we could not see any channel markers. After a couple of minutes idling out, we ran aground. I reluctantly got out, and pushed us back into the channel. The other boat called on the radio, and said they were going to anchor until the fog lifted because they could not see the channel markers at all. The man I was with made some comment, but just kept moving. We ran aground, and I pushed us back into the channel again. Finally, he got the idea it was too foggy to continue, and we anchored until the sun burned some of the fog off.

Sometimes, we can feel like our lives are covered with a fog. No matter what we do, we just seem to keep running aground, unable to see the channel markers. All the little Christian quotes people throw out seem to mean nothing, and the fog only seems to get thicker. We needed to anchor that day, and wait until the sun burned off some of the fog. Maybe you are in a place in your life where you need to anchor for a while until the "Son" clears away some of the fog. To continue blindly on when you are not able to determine where you are going can bring disaster. Anchoring for a while can allow the Holy Spirit time to bring God's will and direction into view.

Hebrews 12:2, “Fixing our eyes on Jesus, the pioneer and perfecter of faith.”

New Rope in the Garage?

I had gotten a fantastic deal on the half-inch braided anchor line. I decided to make two equal lengths of 150 feet, so it would be easier to handle. Because it was new, and looked so good, I decided to save it until later. That was three years ago. I was now looking through my stuff, and deciding what to sell at the garage sale. As I looked at the new rope I had never used; I knew I needed to make a decision. I decided to put the old anchor rope in the garage sale, and place the new rope in the boat. The old rope was still usable, but why waste the new rope by allowing it to just sit in the garage, not being utilized.

What has God done recently in your life that you have left in the garage to be used at a more convenient time? Has God spoken into your heart about teaching a class, sharing your testimony, or maybe even writing a book, but you have simply put that desire on the shelf, waiting for another time? It is too easy to fall into a comfort zone where we are fearful of making changes, or even allowing the Holy Spirit to bring something new into our lives.

Just as the old rope was still working for me, what you are doing may seem to be okay. Is it what God has planned next for your life? You may not need to put anything from your life into a garage sale, but you may need to allow the Holy Spirit to use that new thing He has been birthing in your spirit.

Isaiah 43:19a, "See, I am doing a new thing! Now it springs up; do you not perceive it?"

Stand on Your Commitments

The name of my boat is "Never on Sunday," because as a pastor, I have committed to the Lord to never take the boat out on Sunday. Over the years, the name has gotten me some unusual comments. One day, as I was getting fuel, a classy-looking lady got out of a fancy car, and called to me, "Hey, what's with the name on the boat?" I told her that, as a pastor, I made a commitment when I bought the boat not to take it out on Sunday. She promptly replied, "There is nothing wrong with going out on a boat on Sunday," and walked away. I didn't say there was anything wrong with it, only that "I" had made a commitment not to.

A short time later, I was launching the boat at the ramp, and an elderly gentleman was launching his kayak. He mentioned the name on the boat, and then remarked, "You must be a godly man." I explained to him that, as a pastor, I had committed to the Lord that I would not take the boat out on Sunday. That led us to talking about church, and how much he enjoyed being a part of the family of God.

You can be assured when you make a commitment to God about something in your life, you will also find those who strongly question your reasoning. Others will quickly affirm your decision. Even though we do not mean to offend by our decisions, some may be convicted because of the stand we take. Listen to the Lord, and stand on the commitments you make to Him, no matter what people say.

Luke 6:26, "Woe to you when everyone speaks well of you, for that is how their ancestors treated the false prophets."

Encouragement is the Key

I set the hook, and immediately knew that this was a really big fish. We had a friend and his teenage son with us on the boat, so I called Luke over and handed him the rod. I stood close to encourage him, and offer advice as he struggled to get the fish up from the bottom. After several minutes of reeling, we saw color as the seven-foot shark came near the surface.

As adults, you and I have a great responsibility to teach and encourage the younger generation in the things of life...especially as it relates to their walk with Christ. We need to take time to let them be a part of what we do, not just expect them to watch and learn. They may not always do it exactly as we do, and it may not always come out the way we wanted. We can be an encouragement to them, and even offer gentle wisdom and advice as they work their way through the situation. It is easy for many of us to criticize and complain about this younger generation, when, in reality, we've done little to help and encourage them.

The look on Luke's face, as the shark came alongside the boat, made it all worthwhile. I felt the joy he was feeling, and was rewarded with a generous thank you and an enormous smile on his face.

It's time we do more than just complain about what is not being done by the younger generation. We need to hand them the rod occasionally, and encourage and help them as they learn to fish for themselves.

Judges 3:2, "He did this only to teach warfare to the descendants of the Israelites who had not had previous battle experience."

More than Just Casual Friends

I arrived a few minutes early at the boat ramp, and launched the boat. Three men that I had met at our neighborhood garage sale were to meet me for a day of fishing. They arrived shortly, and began bringing their gear to the boat. The first man to speak to me only said a few words, before letting me know that he had won his first person to the Lord the past week. I did not know that any of the men were Christians, so his comment caught me somewhat by surprise. I told him I was a pastor, and, immediately, we were talking as if we had known each other for a long time.

To say we are brothers in Christ should mean far more than we simply are a part of the Body of Christ. It should bring a special relationship, fostered by the same love in our hearts for others that Christ had. God has grafted us into His family, and calls us the children of God. The church should be a place where those of like faith can experience fellowship with others within the body of Christ. Everyone around them should sense it. The last place in the world we should see or hear of discord and infighting is in the Church, the Body of Christ.

It was a great day on the water fishing, because I had met a brother in Christ I had not known before. I was grateful for his willingness to share his faith, and it made our time together more special.

John 13:35, "By this, everyone will know that you are My disciples, if you love one another." We need to let our love for each other show continually.

Mutual Interest Opens Doors

Our community garage sale was going very well, and we were enjoying the opportunity to meet people we would never have met, otherwise. I had set about eight fishing rods out to sell, and it seemed that every man that walked up to our sale would stop and begin looking at the rods. That was my opportunity to engage them in conversation by asking, "Do you like to fish?" Often, we would then be talking for the next few minutes about various aspects of fishing. I had a chance to ask a few of them if they would like to join me sometime for a fishing trip.

The talents and skills God has blessed us with, even the hobbies we love, should be seen as a way to engage people in conversations that can open a door for letting them know about our love for Christ. I usually let them know that the name of my boat is "Never on Sunday," and that opens another door of conversation. I have discovered, almost without exception, that when I begin a conversation based on a mutual like, or interest, I will have a great opportunity to bring up the name of Christ without offense to the person I am talking with.

What skills or interest has God given you that could be the key to a conversation with someone who needs to hear about Christ? Let the Holy Spirit guide you. Use something you are fond of, or familiar with, to open up a conversation. You will find, in most cases, your words about Christ will be better received when you have said something that makes you accepted.

Proverbs 15:23, "A person finds joy in giving an apt reply, and how good is a timely word!"

Don't Blame Everyone Else

We were following the channel in from a day of fishing, when we saw the large center console flying across a very shallow area, heading toward the dock. Even in the "no wake" zone, he never slowed down. When we reached the dock, the bow of the boat was nosed up to the sand, instead of tied to the dock. As we approached, the two young men moved the boat from the sand to the dock. They called over that they had to tie up there, because they were pumping water out of the bilge. Apparently, the boat had begun taking on water offshore. I asked them what happened, and they said, "The plug fell out." Being an experienced boater, I knew the plug had not " fallen out," but someone had forgotten to put it in.

How often, in our spiritual lives, we are quick to blame someone, or something, for the situation we find ourselves in. In reality, a bad decision on our part is the real culprit. We fail to get the promotion at work, and we blame someone, when we know that we never put in the kind of effort necessary to earn it. We find ourselves struggling financially, but we never consider that our credit card use may be to blame. Our grades in school are always the fault of a poor teacher, and our marital problems are the spouse's fault. Anything, or anyone, except us, is to blame. I'm glad the young men got back in safely, but unless they make sure the plug is in the next time, they will have the problem again.

Genesis 3:12, "The man said, 'The woman you put here with me ...she gave me some fruit from the tree, and I ate it.'"

What are They Looking For?

I nosed the boat up to the buoy, marking the place where I had dropped the three pinfish traps the day before. We were looking forward to having live bait for our day of offshore fishing. As we pulled the first trap in, we realized there were no pinfish in it. The same was true with the second and the third. I was puzzled, because we had placed the traps a couple of weeks before in the same area, and had over 50 pinfish. As we were running out to our first number, I was thinking about what might have happened, and realized that I had used different bait two weeks before.

We get discouraged when the ministry we are involved in seems to be missing the mark. What we are doing just doesn't seem to have the effectiveness that it had before, and is not drawing people the way it once did. As I found that day, just doing the same thing, or placing the traps in the same place, did not necessarily mean I would be successful in catching the pinfish. I needed to make sure the bait I was using was what they were looking for.

If your ministry is lacking something, make sure what you are offering is what your target is looking for. It sounds good and looks good to you, but do the people you are trying to reach have any interest? Ministry today is so much about compassion... meeting people right where they are hurting. Check your bait. Does it include a heart of compassion?

Mark 1:41, "And Jesus, moved with compassion, put forth His hand, and touched him, and said unto him, I will; be thou clean."

Just Try the Old Grouper Trick

I had just set the grouper rod with the 4" live pinfish in the rod holder when the clicker began to scream. I quickly put the reel in gear, and set the hook on the fish. I had no idea what had hit, but it was large and headed toward the front of the boat. I maneuvered around Mike, and moved to follow the fish. Suddenly, the movement stopped, and I realized the fish had somehow gotten back into its hole. I pulled several times, but to no avail. I told Mike I was going to give the fish some slack, and just wait a few minutes to see what might happen.

Sometimes, we have put a great deal of effort into doing all the right things to bring someone to Christ. Something happens, and they suddenly seem to take off, running from you, and what you know God wants to do in their life. It may seem they have reached a place where no matter what you say, they will not move. Many an individual has been pushed away, because we were afraid "we" would lose them for the Lord if we didn't keep pressing in. Try the old grouper trick; give them a little slack, all the while praying that the Holy Spirit will do the work only He is capable of doing. The Holy Spirit will let you know when to check the line again.

When I picked up the rod a few minutes later, the 27" gag grouper was out of his hole, and I was able to bring him to the net.

Proverbs 25:17, "Seldom set foot in your neighbor's house — too much of you, and they will hate you. Don't wear out your welcome; be patient."

Always Room For Compassion

As I watched the news report, I could hardly believe what I saw. The gambling boat ferry, that was often docked where I launch my boat, was making its morning run out to the gambling ship. As it rounded the marker to leave the Cotee River, and make its way offshore, a fire started and quickly spread on the boat. The captain acted quickly to nose the large boat into shallow water. The people on board quickly began to jump off the bow into the chilly shallow water and make their way to the shore. The houses there, in a gated community, are very expensive, but the homeowners quickly began to respond by helping them get to the shore. Others were rushing out of their homes with blankets, towels, or whatever else they could find.

My heart was touched with the response from those homeowners. It would have been easy to just look the other way, and not get involved in the situation. There was no loss of life that day, because of the quick actions of the captain, and the compassionate response of the people on shore.

We should also be quick to respond with compassion to those who may find themselves in a bad situation. Our Lord never said, "I don't want to get involved. We should never say that, either. We may be limited in some ways as to what we can do, but that limitation should never be determined by our lack of compassion for those in need. Trust the Holy Spirit to give you strength.

Mark 6:34a, "And Jesus, when He came out, saw much people, and was moved with compassion toward them."

The Warning is for a Reason

The fellows stepped on board, and we left the dock just a few minutes before the sunrise. As we idled out the channel, the heat indicator on the engine sounded, warning that the engine was getting hotter than normal. I put the motor in neutral, and stepped to the back of the boat to see if water was coming out of the indicator tube on the motor. The stream was very weak, so I told the men that we needed to head back to the dock. Of course, everyone was disappointed, but it was better to discover the problem now than latter when we were several miles out. Just as I reached the dock, the heat indicator stopped beeping. I saw that the engine temperature was back to normal. We let the engine idle a few minutes, then decided to continue our trip out.

It can be disastrous, and sometimes costly, to barrel ahead in life when a spiritual indicator light is going off in our spirits. The better part of wisdom is to stop, take stock of what is going on, and what the Spirit of God may be speaking to your heart. Often, it does not mean a no, but simply a short delay in what God is working in our life. It may simply mean that God wants you to learn to heed the warnings that come when we may be heading in the wrong direction.

I later discovered that the thermostat was sticking, and the fix was minor. To continue that day without checking things would have been very foolish.

Acts 16:7, "When they came to the border of Mysia, they tried to enter Bithynia, but the Spirit of Jesus would not allow them to." Be sensitive to the Spirit and be safe.

Erosion Can Ruin Your Beauty

I pointed the boat toward the sand bar north of Anclote Island, as I had done with Susan many times before. This is one of our favorite places to walk the shoreline and hunt shells. As we approached the sandbar, I quickly realized that it was noticeably smaller than our last visit. Effects of the wind and the erosion of the waves had taken their toll on the sandbar to the extent that it was less than one-fourth the size it was before. We both remarked about the size, and wondered how much longer there would be a place to come and pick up shells.

It is sometimes easy to forget that our relationship with Christ can begin to erode, just as the sandbar had. The constant pressure from life, and the situations we must struggle through, can have the same effect spiritually on our lives as the waves had on the sandbar. Unlike the sandbar, though, you and I can do something to remedy the problem. Taking the time to assess our spiritual lives will usually show us where we have let down our spiritual guard, and where we need to shore up our relationship with Christ. Erosion, in our spiritual lives, comes when we have neglected to properly maintain through prayer, study of the Word, and quality fellowship with the people of God.

Just as the sandbar attracted people because of what it offered, the beauty of Christ in us should also attract people. Don't allow the erosion of the world to rob you of your beauty in Christ.

Matthew 5:16, "In the same way, let your light shine before others, that they may see your good deeds and glorify your Father in Heaven."

The Blue Smoke is Gone

If you remember the outboard motors of yesteryear, you may remember they were difficult to start, noisy, and produced a lot of smoke when started. The smoke was because the gas and oil was mixed together, and the burning oil produced the smoke. The new engines today are a far cry from those noisy gas-guzzling smokers. Today's engines are efficient, clean burning, and very reliable. When they are started, they produce no smoke, you can hardly hear them running, and they are very dependable.

We often see the same truth in the lives of Christians. When they first come to know the Lord, their life and walk with God can be anything but smooth and dependable. Traits of the "old man" are still encountered when they face trials or temptations. I know I have seen a little smoke coming from them, as they face the challenges. The same should not be true of those who have walked with God for a greater period of time. Their ability to handle the trials and temptations of life should be seen as smoother and more efficient. Their consistency in the faith should mark them as people who have spent quality time with the Lord, and have grown in the process. The new outboards are not perfect, but they have come a long way from their inception. We may not be perfect, but if we have known the Lord for a few years, it should easily be detected. The outboard industry has made improvements that are easily seen in their new products. Growth in our walk and relationship with Christ should be easily seen, also..

2 Peter 3:18, "But grow in the grace and knowledge of our Lord and Savior Jesus Christ."

Seas Two Feet or Less

There is a standing joke between my son, Kenny, and me. When I am going off shore, I usually tell him, "The seas are two feet or less." Of course, that is not always the case when we get out there. I have been out on days when there was literally not a ripple on the water. I have been on the Gulf in five to seven foot seas, as well. The conditions are subject to change, just as quickly as the weather changes.

The same is true in our lives. We can have a time when there is not a ripple in life. Everything is going smoothly, and there are no problems or difficulties. Things can change in a very short period of time. From calm and smooth conditions, our lives can suddenly be thrown into turmoil and troubles that we never saw coming. You might receive a diagnosis from the doctor, a notice of divorce proceedings from a spouse, or you find your child is on drugs, or pregnant and unmarried. The seas of life are no longer "two feet or less." The calm of life has turned into a raging sea of pain and heartbreak.

These are the times that we must put our trust and confidence in the Master of the winds, the waves, and the sea. Just as Jesus commanded the winds and waves to be still for the disciples, He can command the circumstances of your life. The conditions you are facing may not change right away, but Christ can bring a peace to your heart, as you put your trust Him.

Mark 4:39, "He got up, rebuked the wind, and said to the waves, 'Quiet! Be still.' Then the wind died down, and it was completely calm."

Don’t Give Up on That Boat

As I looked at the boat in the yard, I knew it had sunk in a storm several years before, and the owner had left it unattended sense then. I was looking for a small boat, and felt that it had potential. The process would take several weeks, but, with time and effort, I replaced the rotten wood in the transom, the soft spots in the floor, and I got the engine running again. A new paint job followed the repairs, new seats were installed, and I was now sitting in the boat on the lake ready to make its inaugural run. Those looking on that day at this little beauty had no idea that it was once underwater for hours, was neglected for several years, and had not run during that entire time. How many of our lives could tell a similar story today? Many were brought up in a broken or an abusive home by parents or others who paid little or no attention to them. They were fed lies about who they were or could be, and the future ahead of them looked hopeless. God found them in His grace, and began to allow the Holy Spirit to do His incredible work in their hearts and lives. When people see the spiritual beauty they have become, as they serve in our churches and in the Kingdom of God, few would ever guess what God has accomplished in their life.

Just like I saw the potential in that little boat, God sees the potential in the saddest of situations, and He is able to make all the necessary repairs.

Philippians 1:6, “Being confident of this, that He who began a good work in you will carry it on to completion until the day of Christ Jesus.”

I Can Handle Whatever You Do

As I pressed the throttle lever forward on the boat, the rope quickly became tight on the large inner tube behind us. My friend had remarked only a few minutes before that no one could throw him off the tube. I was quite confident that no matter how strong he thought he was, I knew something he did not know. As the boat moved faster and faster, I began turning in a tight and continuous circle. The tube was skipping across the water at an ever increasing speed. It was then that I moved the boat out of the circle, allowing the tube to be drawn through the large wake the turning boat had created. When it hit the large wake, it quickly became airborne. As the tube became airborne, the heavy side of the tube, with my friend clinging to it, rolled over, becoming the bottom side of the now flying tube. When it hit the water again, my friend was quickly extracted from the speeding tube.

We can sometimes become self-confident and prideful in our walk with Christ. That self-confidence can lead us to make choices and decisions that we are sure that we can handle. The problem is the enemy may know something we do not know. He is often waiting for this prideful opportunity to bring something into our lives that we never expected.

Just as my friend had no idea what my plans were to dislodge him from the tube, we may never see coming what the enemy has planned for us. Don't allow self-confidence to cause you to be vulnerable to the attack of the enemy.

2 Corinthians 3:5, "Not that we are competent in ourselves to claim anything for ourselves, but our competence comes from God."

Unseen Problems Can Cost You

Mike was enjoying a day on the water with us. It had been several weeks since he had been fishing, so this was a real treat for him. He had brought his own rod and reel that he had used many times before. As he continued catching fish, he suddenly commented that something seemed to be wrong with the reel. As we checked it out, we found two of the screws that held the reel to the mounting bracket had apparently worked loose and the reel was in danger of coming off the rod. The screws were on the inside of the reel where you could not see when they worked loose. To make a repair would require taking the reel apart, and refastening the screws in place.

How many times have we discovered that some area of our lives in Christ seems to be coming apart, and after checking things out, we find something going on off our normal radar screen? We are usually careful about the obvious spiritual maintenance, but often do not pay enough attention to those areas which are less noticeable. We are careful about what we say and do, but often allow our minds to wander dangerously. We are careful about the friends we keep, but do not seem to notice that what we are reading or looking at is out of line.

Those four small screws holding the reel to the bracket could not even be seen from the outside of the reel, but without them the reel was in danger of falling off the rod.

Don't allow the "little foxes to spoil your reel."

Song of Solomon 2:15 , "Catch for us the foxes, the little foxes that ruin the vineyards. They may be small, but they are not insignificant."

Check the Radar First

One of the most important preparation disciplines to enjoying a day on the water is to be very aware of the weather conditions. When planning a trip offshore, I start looking at the weather report five or six days in advance to see if the weather will be good. I continue to watch as the day approaches for the trip. I even get up early on the day of the planned trip, and look at the local radar and read the weather report before making the final decision. With the weather technology available to us, there is no excuse to be caught unaware of a weather situation that could be dangerous.

The same is true in our Christian walk. The word of God is like spiritual weather technology. God has given us His word to warn us of areas of danger, so that we can avoid them. He warns us of inappropriate relationships... the sky may seem clear now, but storm clouds are moving in. We really have no excuse to be caught unaware of the devices of the enemy, if we utilize the word of God to determine the spiritual weather that can adversely affect us.

We have all read of individuals who venture out on the water and get caught by bad weather, losing life and property? If we heed the weather warnings of Scripture, we will prevent many of the situations that are designed by the enemy to swamp our vessel and destroy our lives. Before you make that decision, check the spiritual weather radar in God's Word.

Psalms 119:37, "Turn my eyes away from worthless things; preserve my life according to Your Word."

Rest a While, Don't Just Quit

Jim had driven over to Cedar Key to join my Dad, my brother and me, for a day of offshore fishing. We had left the dock early, and made the fifteen mile run to one of my favorite locations. We dropped our lines over the side, and almost as soon as the baits hit the bottom, we were hooked up on fish. Bill was especially having a great time, as he reeled in fish after fish, sometimes two at the time on the double hook rigs we were using. Almost an hour into it, I heard Bill say, "My arm is killing me, I don't think I can pull in another fish." He put the rod back into the holder, and just sat back watching the rest of us, as we continued to catch fish. In a few minutes, I saw him pick up the rod again. When he caught me looking at him, he said, "I can't stand watching all of you catch fish and not fish myself."

When is the last time you became weary doing something for the Lord and decided to quit? Maybe you laid aside the call of God on your life, because you felt like you did not have the strength to go on or deal with another situation. A little rest is alright, and may do a world of good. Don't allow the enemy, however, to rob you of the joy of working for the Lord. Pick up the rod again, and put the bait back in the water. God's still wants to use you to minister in His Kingdom.

Galatians 6:9, "Let us not become weary in doing good, for at the proper time we will reap a harvest if we do not give up."

The Value of Proper Anchoring

Having a good knowledge and understanding of the equipment on your boat, and how it works, can help you have a safe, fun-filled day on the water. Most states do not require licenses to own or operate a boat. Consequently, many people on the water may not have a good knowledge of the proper and safe operation of their vessel. The proper use of one piece of equipment on the boat, often taken for granted, is the anchor. A good understanding and use of the anchor can make a big difference. When properly set and attached to the bow of the boat, the anchor can hold the boat securely, allowing it to ride the waves safely. In rough water, anchoring the boat from the stern can place the boat in danger of the waves breaking over the transom, as the stern is not designed to handle those waves.

The same is true for those whose lives are anchored to a difficult or painful situation in their past. Old hurts, relationship problems, maybe even a marriage gone badly, can be a dangerous place to have our life anchored. The conflicts and memories associated with the past can make waves that have the capacity to fill our life with bitterness, anger, unforgiveness, hopelessness, or other weights that will swamp what God wants to do in our lives.

When we anchor our lives to the leading of Christ, we stay bow on to life's waves that confront us, and we can ride out every situation. If you find your life being swamped by things from the past, check the location of your anchor connection.

Hebrews 6:19, "We have this hope as an anchor for the soul, firm and secure."

Radio Is Useless if Not On

An important piece of safety equipment on a boat is the VHF radio. This radio uses wireless technology to communicate across distances on the water. It allows boaters who may be facing an emergency to call for help, or notify someone of their location. The problem comes when you may be too far from land to be picked up by those monitoring the emergency channel 16. The only way to get help then, or notify someone of the emergency you are in, is to reach another boat close to your location that can relay your message. Unfortunately, many boaters fail to turn on their radio unless they need it, and others, even when they turn it on, fail to monitor the emergency channel.

When you or I find our lives in a spiritual emergency, we also may need to contact someone who can respond to us. Just like many boaters, many Christians live in the body of Christ with their spiritual sensitivity to others turned off. They may be so caught up in their own situations that they fail to hear or sense the emergency going on around them. God intended the Church to be a place where those facing an emergency in their lives could call on other believers to help them overcome whatever they were facing. I assure you, there is an SOS signal going out from someone around you right now.

Turn on your spiritual radio. Locate the emergency frequency, and listen closely. Someone may be seeking help.

2 Corinthians 1:4, "Who comforts us in all our troubles, so that we can comfort those in any trouble with the comfort we ourselves receive from God."

What Are We Attracting?

I get the same question almost every time I take someone new on the boat with me out the Cotee River. They see the small frame houses on poles in the water, just outside the mouth of the river. The houses were apparently placed there years ago, before the environmentalists and others had rules against it. They are allowed to remain now, but very little repair or upgrades are ever made. Sometimes you see people there on the weekend, but, there is no power available, so living there on a regular basis is not feasible. There are some permanent residents, however. The pelicans, sea gulls, and other water birds roost there almost constantly. Many times, when the wind is blowing just right, the smell can be quite noxious.

Sometimes, we can allow the same to happen in our Christian lives. We have a presence in the kingdom of God, but because we have not taken the time to maintain our walk and relationship with Christ, we find our relationship with Him, and the church, going downhill fast. You can even find the pelicans, sea gulls, and other water fowls of this world roosting in areas of your life, because the real presence of the Holy Spirit is seldom there.

What do people notice when they see your life in Christ? The small houses at the mouth of the Cotee River attract attention, but they have little usefulness and the smell is not conducive to attracting visitors. Let's pray that something better can be said of our lives in Christ.

Matthew 5:16, "In the same way, let your light shine before others, that they may see your good deeds and glorify your Father in heaven."

What Holds Your Anchor Fast?

One of the most important pieces of equipment on a boat is the anchor. It is the device needed to hold your boat in position when you are not near enough to land or a dock to tie it off. The anchor comes in many sizes and shapes, determined by what kind of boat you own, the size of the boat, depth of the water, and the kind of bottom you will be using it in most often. This is not a "one size fits all" piece of equipment.

Deploying or setting the anchor also involves a certain amount of skill, and done improperly, your boat will drift off location, possibly causing damage to it or other boats anchored close by. Although we call it an anchor, by itself it has little ability to keep us in place. Every anchor is only as good as what it can lodge itself in to hold your boat.

When we examine our lives in Christ, we need an anchor, and that anchor is the faith that we possess. All the faith in the world, however, is useless unless we have a place for it to sink into. There are many around the world that believe, and even have faith in what they believe, but that faith does not have a secure place for the anchor to hold. Our faith must be solidly affixed in the Word of God and Jesus Christ, if it is to hold securely in the waves and currents we are confronted with in this world.

Don't be fooled into thinking that it is only important to believe or have faith. The anchor must have a place that is secure if it is to hold.

Hebrew 6:19, "We have this hope as an anchor for the soul, firm and secure."

The Slime is for a Reason

I brought the salt water catfish into the boat, and used a towel to hold it firmly. I removed the hook, and threw the catfish back in the water. I noticed the towel had a thick, slimy residue from the fish. All fish have some coating, and there are good reasons for it. The slime coating is the first line of defense for the fish against bacteria and parasites in the water. Knowledgeable fishermen will carefully handle a game fish, so that this slime coat is not removed from the fish, endangering it. Other things, such as water quality, water temperature, and stress on the fish because of other aggressive fish, can also affect this coating.

When we come to Christ, we receive the Holy Spirit who acts as a "protective coating" in our lives. He is there to help guard us against parasites and bacteria from this world that would try to infect our spiritual lives. Many Christians have had their spiritual lives damaged by ill treatment of fellow believers. Harsh, unkind words, or criticism, may remove some of the "protective coating," exposing them to parasites and bacteria of anger, discouragement, bitterness, and doubt.

We must be careful how we handle each other. As believers, we need to be careful we do not put ourselves in places where our protective coating can be adversely affected by choices and surroundings. The coating on the fish can be replenished, but the fish will be in danger until that takes place.

1 Corinthians 8:9, "Be careful, however, that the exercise of your rights does not become a stumbling block to the weak."

That Additive Can Cost You

You may have noticed the signs at gas stations that advertise "Ethanol Free" gas. This is directed mostly to people who own boats. The ethanol that is being added to gasoline in our country can be very damaging to a boat's engine and fuel system. Many boats have a fiberglass constructed gas tank, and the resin of the fiberglass can break down somewhat when alcohol is present. The resin can then get into delicate fuel systems, and clog up important parts in the engine. What seemed like a great idea has become a serious problem to many boat owners.

The enemy has a way of interjecting things into our lives that may seem good at the time, but they can begin to breakdown and clog up our spiritual life-line to the Lord. That new friend who tends to pull you from your commitment to Christ, or that new hobby that is robbing you of precious time with the Lord, even a new promotion that takes you away from home and the church... all these, and many others, can clog our spiritual lives. They all may start without any obvious ill effects, but, given an opportunity, they can break down and ruin what God has designed for us. We need to be mindful that the decisions we make need to be carefully thought through, and we get an approval from the Lord for the choices we are making.

Ethanol is less than 10% by volume in gasoline, but that 10% can cost a boat owner thousands of dollars in repair. Your choice today may seem trivial, in the scheme of things, but what will it ultimately cost you?

Galatians 5:9, "A little yeast works through the whole batch of dough."

Don't Believe It's the Bottom

I set the hook attached to the 80 Lb line and the heavy rod and reel, but it felt like I was hung up on the bottom. I pulled hard on the line, but I realized that something was pulling against me. This was a fish, but it was bigger than anything I had ever caught before. I was putting all the tension on the fish the rod would take, but I couldn't move it. One of the men on the boat said, "You're hung on the bottom." but I assured him that was not true. I continued to pull on the rod until the huge ten-foot nurse shark came to the surface. I pulled it alongside the boat, took several pictures, and finally released it. I was exhausted from the fight, but I could not have been happier.

We can have those same feelings as God calls on us to accept a spiritual challenge in our lives. When we begin the process, we may feel that it is an impossible task, and there may even be those who discount the value of what you feel God has called you to do. If you know God has spoken to your heart, don't give up...just go for it. Keep pulling, keep straining, and keep working at it.

A ten-foot fish may be the largest fish I am ever privileged to catch, but I know, if given the opportunity for a bigger one, I will give it my all. You may not know what God has ahead for you, but be resolved to always give it your best, and God will do the rest. God's call is more than a dream, it's a promise.

2 Corinthians 1:20, "For no matter how many promises God has made, they are "Yes" in Christ."

About the Author

Ken Pippin was born in a rural section of the panhandle of north Florida, but his family moved to the Tampa area when he was five years old. His mom and dad instilled in him at a very young age the value of a relationship with Jesus Christ, and also the importance of serving the Lord with his life. After graduating high school, Ken met the girl that would become his wife at the age of nineteen. After their marriage, in 1968, Ken was promoted to management with Winn-Dixie Supermarkets. He and Susan were blessed with two boys while he worked for Winn-Dixie, and served in Glad Tidings Assembly of God, Tampa, Florida. At age twenty six, he joined the Tampa Fire Department, and achieved the rank of Captain, with his own station, in ten years. He continued to serve the church during this time, but he and Susan began to feel the call of God for full time ministry as pastors. In October of 1985, he resigned from the Tampa Fire Department, and they accepted a small church in Keystone Heights, Florida, serving there until June of 2002. During that time, they were blessed to build a new sanctuary and burn the mortgage. After much prayer and listening for the voice of God, they resigned their church, and moved to Tarpon Springs, Florida, in June of 2002, to accept the position as lead pastors of Highest Praise Family Church. God would once again stretch them, as they would again build a new sanctuary at the main location. They started a satellite church, in Port Richey, designed to minister to a large community of homeless individuals. In January of 2014, Ken was asked to assume a position with the Peninsular Florida District. He continued to pastor full time, but soon realized that God was leading them to resign as pastors in order to give more time to the new ministry. They resigned the church in December of 2016, and began serving full time as the Director of Adult Ministries.

Made in the USA
Monee, IL
18 January 2021

56602550R00148